Cultural Icons

Cultural Icons

Keyan G. Tomaselli and David Scott, Editors

Left Coast Press Inc.

Walnut Creek, California

LEFT COAST PRESS, INC.
1630 North Main Street, #400
Walnut Creek, California 94596
http://www.lcoastpress.com

Copyright © 2009 by Intervention Press

Hardback ISBN 978-1-59874-365-4
Paperback ISBN 978-1-59874-366-1

Paperback edition published outside of the Americas under
ISBN 978-87-89825-53-3 by:
Intervention Press
Castenschioldsvej 7
DK-8270 Hoejbjerg
Denmark
www.intervention.dk

Library of Congress Cataloging-in-Publication Data
Cultural icons / Keyan Tomaselli and David Scott, editors.
    p. cm.
    Includes index.
    ISBN 978-1-59874-365-4 (hardcover : alk. paper) – ISBN 978-1-59874-366-1 (pbk.: alk. paper)
    1. Culture. 2. Visual perception. 3. Art and society. I. Tomaselli, Keyan G., 1948- II. Scott, David.
    HM621.C852 2008
    306.4'2—dc22   2008049707

09 10 11 5 4 3 2 1

Printed in the United States of America

♾™ The paper used in this publication meets the minimum requirements of American National Standard for Information Sciences—Permanence of Paper for Printed Library Materials, ANSI/NISO Z39.48—1992.

Cover design by: Andrew Brozyna

CONTENTS

ACKNOWLEDGMENTS

The editors would like to thank Hans Lund and Bernhard Scholtz for the groundwork done on this project, which resulted in a workshop of potential authors held in 2000 at the Litteraturvetenskapliga Institutionen, Lunds Universitet, Sweden. Our thanks also go to Trinity College, Dublin, and the University of KwaZulu-Natal (UKZN), for funding that enabled us to complete the project. Thanks also to Diedre Donnelly (also for UKZN) who prepared the manuscript for publication, and to Diedre Donnelly, Anusha Govender, and Simone Samuels who assisted with copy editing.

INTRODUCTION: CULTURAL ICONS

David Scott and Keyan G. Tomaselli

What is meant by *culture*, and specifically what is cultural studies? What is the study of visual culture? And finally, what is an icon, and in our case, a cultural icon? The first section of this chapter situates the specific studies that follow within a general framing of cultural studies. The relationship between cultural studies and visual culture is then briefly teased out. Finally, our use of the term *cultural icons* is examined in the second section of this introduction as it relates to the book as a whole.

Cultural Studies: Visualizing Culture

Each of the essays that make up this volume on cultural icons in their own different ways fall into the general category of cultural studies and also, though less generally, into the more recent and specific branch of cultural studies that is now known as visual culture. Before turning briefly to comment on the more specific orientation of this volume with reference to the different cultural icons studied within it, we will first make an attempt to situate this project in a more general way within the wider field of contemporary visual and cultural studies. We will also assess both the theoretical bases and the methodological approaches adopted by these areas of study.

First, then, what is cultural studies? Cultural studies seems broadly to have emerged in the mid-1950s as a result, first, of a certain dissatisfaction with the response of traditional disciplines of the arts and humanities such as art history and literature to the questions posed both by and within contemporary culture, and, second, of a need both to exploit and to critique the possibilities opened up to the arts and humanities of linguistic, semiotic, and other innovative approaches to cultural analysis. Culture was increasingly interpreted after the 1880s in a normative and inclusive way as "the best that is thought and done in a society," including within its ambit morals, art, law, and so on (cf. Arnold 1966; Tylor 1924). However, with the growth of mass society during the first part of the twentieth century, a more critically inclusive approach emerged – one that not only brought together the insights of the different arts and humanities disciplines into new interdisciplinary frames but also implied the creation of new forms of interdiscipline, offering new sites of study that included the popular and the political. This latter distinction would be in particular a function of the theoretical reflection that would necessarily inform the new approaches adopted by cultural studies and visual culture. The particular challenges of a cultural studies approach that is explicitly mobilized via semiotics, are, first, its wide-ranging scope. Semiotics/semiology is the study of how signs (visual, aural, linguistic) take on meaning where the sign *stands for* something else. For example a photograph of the Eiffel Tower stands for the real thing, the metal structure located in Paris. Jonathan Culler, who from the 1970s was one of the earliest and most influential proponents of structuralist and linguistically derived semiological approaches to studies in the arts and humanities, comments, "Culture is, on the one hand, the system of categories and assumptions that makes possible the activities and productions of a society and, on the other hand, the products themselves, so the reach of cultural studies is vast" (quoted in Bal 1999: 337).

Culler stresses the intrinsically theoretical turn implied by cultural studies when he writes that "cultural studies can be the study of anything whatsoever, when it is made theoretically interesting" (Bal 1999: 340). He argues that "cultural studies is the practice of which what we call 'theory' is the theory" (Bal 1999: 341) and that "cultural analysis [is] the site where the reflexivity that ought to characterize all disciplines takes place" (Bal 1999: 346). Reflexivity returns the emphasis to a discussion of method, semiotics, and the like. If cultural studies is the theory of theory, then its appropriation of semiotics as a method of methods inevitably fixes the theory-method that is cultural studies into a transdisciplinary realm.

The second major challenge facing cultural studies is clearly identified by Simon During: "Cultural studies is a discipline continuously shifting its interests and methods both because it is in constant and engaged interaction with its larger historical context and because it cannot be complacent about is authority" (During 1999: 18). Semiotics is at the heart of cultural studies and visual culture because it is, first, about representation within a given society or ethos, or, increasingly, within a transnational world, across a heterogeneous range of receivers in the global village; and, second, because of the necessity to *reflect upon* problems of representation and to submit representation to analysis within a coherent theoretical framework. As During confirms, "engaged cultural studies . . . examines its own constitutive borders and divisions" (During 1999: 25), a position echoed by Mieke Bal when she argues that "methodological explicitness is one feature of cultural analysis" (1999: 4) and that "cultural analysis [is] inherently self-reflexive" (1999: 6). As Foucault pointed out already in *Les Mots et les choses* (1966), semiotics within the Western tradition may be considered as englobing two potentialities that struggle to become unified: *semiology* and *hermeneutics*. These two potentialities in their dialectical tension constitute culture: how do groups and classes of people make sense of their respective worlds? Semiology is "l'ensemble des connaissances et des techniques qui permettent de distinguer où sont les signes" [the sum of knowledge and techniques that enables signs to be apprehended] while *hermeneutics* is 'l'ensemble des connaissances et des techniques qui permettent de faire parler les signes et de découvrir leurs sens' [the sum of knowledge and techniques that enable signs to speak and to reveal their meaning] (Foucault 1966: 44). Cultural studies should aim to attend to both the *semiological* (the nature of the sign system; the components around which it is constructed) and the *hermeneutic* (how signs are interpreted; what sort of meanings are produced) aspect of semiotics.

Semiotics, as used in this volume, further draws on the method proposed by Charles Sanders Peirce, which offers a nonlinguistic, antistructuralist contextual foundation to the historical analysis of visual phenomena in particular. *Structuralism* is the generic name of that body of theory that bases itself on the work of Ferdinand de Saussure (1972), and under which semiology is subsumed. The analytical tendency has been to naturalize the structure of difference, proposed as a hypothesis in his work, into a formal "map" onto the grid of which all signs relate in one-to-one correspondence with specific reference points. In these theories, every sign consists of a *signifier* and a *signified* in arbitrary dyadic relationships that signify by virtue of their *difference to other such pairs*. In terms of this logic, we are imprisoned in a world of linguistic structures. The mess and confusion found in everyday life, to use Husserl's (1969) term, are "bracketed out" because they obscure the clarity of the structure; the realization of this was ultimately to lead to the unpicking, or "deconstruction," of the structures. If semiology is itself just such a structure, one could say that trying to "see through" the structure leaves one with nothing to which reference can be made, except possibly some prior structure in a potential infinite regress. This is why all the authors in this volume largely apply a Peircian semiotic, whether explicitly or implicitly, as cultural studies is concerned also with text-context relations, media-society relations, and how meaning is mediated historically via power relations. Also, where semiology is derived from linguistics and is best applied to the study of narrative, Peircian semiotics is better suited to nonlinguistic applications such as the study of the visual.

Cultural studies is not "an archeology of meaning but an interaction with and through meaning that constitutes cultural practice" (Bal 1999: 12–13). It is therefore both inherently inter- and transdisciplinary. Semiotics as an overarching method of methods further facilitates such disciplinary crossings-over. What set Peirce apart from the philosophers of his time was his insistence that science and knowledge are *habits* (or practices) that people develop. These are part of a threefold dynamic process: Peirce saw signs as being *always* iconic, indexical, and symbolic, always subject to the interpretant, the idea to which the sign gives rise (see the Phaneroscopic Table in Chapter 1). The interpretant arises via a triadic process and occurs when an interpreter makes sense of the relation between an object and a sign of that object. The interpreter is always present in what is known as the "stand for" relation, which involves signifier, object, and interpretant. The interpretant locates meaning with the interpreter or interpretive communities, rather than assuming, as does semiology, that meaning resides solely within the dyadic structure of language sans reception by a perceiving being. At its most effective, an interpretant necessarily gives rise to new signs or to new uses of signs, and new sign (or interpretive) communities (new practices). This is known as *unlimited semiotics*. The emergence of the discipline of visual culture out of cultural studies (and art history, among others) is one such habit change or new intellectual practice. There is thus an aspect of *activity* that accompanies a subject's use of signs that makes this triple link the minimum necessary for understanding, since if a sign is to *mean*, then there also has to be at the very least somebody signifying *and* something (an object) that is signified. So, as Bal suggests, "Evolving out of a polemic against the arbitrariness of disciplinary boundaries . . . cultural analysis is truly an interdiscipline, with a specific object and a specific set of collaborating disciplines" (Bal 1999: 6–7). In addition, cultural studies should always take care to situate the object or field of investigation in its historical context, even, as is most often the case in cultural studies, when this happens to be the present. The relationship between cultural studies and history is of course problematic, one of its aims being precisely to problematize "history's silent assumptions" and to understand "the past as *part* of the present" (Bal 1999: 1).

The main components of cultural studies are textual and visual (for our purposes here, aural is subsumed within textual). One emphasis of a semiological and hermeneutically grounded cultural studies, as an interdiscipline, thus poses the question of the nature of the relationship between textual and visual, one that seems to operate within a structure of supplementarity. The West (Europe and America since the sixteenth century) has been a primarily logocentric world in which nature was interpreted through a culture primarily based on language; but within this system visual culture (and in particular, since the Middle Ages, the visual arts) constituted a significant supplement to the logocentric world. But, at the same time, the Logos within the Western tradition may be envisaged as a supplement to nature experienced as a dynamic reality in which visual representation is often closer to the natural world because it is nearer to the iconic end of the scale of symbolic representation. In addition, the visual arts (in particular from the Renaissance onwards) in the form of illustration, "history" painting, or other forms of pictorial representation, pick up and reconfigure the world of the Logos in visual terms. So the supplemental nature of the textual/visual relation is a cyclical one in which one of the two different components from time to time takes precedence over the other but nevertheless always implies or involves the other. In the late twentieth- and early twenty-first-century world, it is language that is tending to become supplemental to the visual image, not least because (as Baudrillard [1981] has shown) culture has become increasingly constructed according to the hyperreal model, through a process of simulation – a situation pithily summarized by Bal as "the stark visuality of present culture" (1999: 9). It is within this stark visuality that cultural icons operate and take their sustenance.

Moving more specifically to visual culture, we note that the term seems to have been first coined by the art historian Svetlana Alpers (1996) when she wrote, "I was not studying the history of Dutch painting, but painting as part of Dutch visual culture." She uses the term in the sense of "a culture in which images, as distinguished from texts, were central to the representation (in the sense of formulation of knowledge) of the world" (Alpers 1996: 26). For an increasing number of art historians contemporary with Alpers, visual culture studies offered a more comprehensive and theoretically sophisticated alternative to traditional art history. As Norman Bryson observes, it marks a shift of focus to "the cultural meaning of the work rather than on its aesthetic value," becoming a history of images rather than history of art (Bryson et al. 1994: xvi). As with cultural studies more generally, visual culture becomes more interdisciplinary in its orientation, offering, as Bryson says, "the prospect of an interdisciplinary dialogue, one that is more concerned with the relevance of contemporary values for academic study than the myth of the pursuit of knowledge for its own sake" (1994: xvii). This broader interdisciplinary project is no longer organized on the model of history but on the model of anthropology (Evans and Hall 1999: 6), a shift that, as Hal Foster observes in

October 77 (1996), as cited by Evans and Hall, "is noteworthy . . . in the displacement of art history by visual culture [and] the dual shift from art to visual, and history to culture" (1999: 6). This shift locates readers, interpreters, and audiences as being central to the meaning-making (semiotic) process. The meaning inferred by an interpreter thus becomes a negotiation between text and context as mediated by interpretants generated by readers.

But the more radical potential of visual culture as a phenomenon and a study area is already brilliantly anticipated by Guy Debord in his seminal book *La Société du spectacle* (1967):

> Toute la vie des sociétés dans lesquelles règnent les conditions modernes de production s'annonce comme une immense accumulation de *spectacles*. Tout ce qui était directement vécu s'est éloigné dans une représentation (1967: 15) [The whole life of societies in which modern conditions of production pertain reveals itself to be a vast agglomeration of spectacle. All directly lived experience becomes distanced from itself through representation].

For Debord, the spectacle is not just a group of images but rather the social relations of individuals as mediated by images. In other words, for Debord, in the society of the spectacle, individuals have less and less contact with the real, whether in terms of the objective world, of other human beings, of themselves, or of their desires. Instead they are fed by a capitalist consumerist environment with substitute images of all these. The spectacle for Debord is thus "le cœur de l' irréalisme de la société réelle" (1967: 17) [the heart of unreality in real society]. Visual culture has since the 1990s made it part of its business to interrogate the mechanisms via which the society of spectacle alienates individuals from their own lives and their environments. The analyses of the post-Marxist sociologist and semiotician Jean Baudrillard in his pioneering works of the 1970s has done much to advance this investigation, in particular in such books as *La Société de consommation* (1970), *Pour une critique de l'économie politique du signe* (1972), *L'Echange symbolique et la mort* (1976), and *Simulacres et simulation* (1981).

The semiology of spectacle slips easily into a world of subjectivist "superstructuralism" wherein practitioners tend to "live" their theories. Thus, at a lecture delivered at New York University in 1978, a dying Roland Barthes turned his (by then) poststructuralist brand of semiology against himself. He had found a barren theoretical prison, his head separate from his body, but with each nevertheless dependent upon the other (see also Jameson 1972). This kind of listless existence of unstable signs, continuously mutating and transforming in unpredictable and surprising ways, seemingly independent of material processes but nevertheless dependent upon them, provides the shifting sands of poststructural thinking. In this mode of trying to make sense, meanings are continuously overturning and being overturned. Barthes therefore had found himself writing within the false security of a structuralist understanding of how meaning is created (i.e., in terms of structures of the mind). After the publication of S/Z (1974), he moved to the insecurity that was born from pulling apart the structuring rules of meaning construction: this led to the deconstruction of even his own structuralist premises. The fading self that was Barthes signified the curse of poststructural semiology because, as Marshall Blonsky (1985: xv) observed, it is "a language with little responsibility towards the real." It becomes a pure idealism or superstructuralism. This process is evident in the way the sign of Nelson Mandela was disarticulated from the material and bloody discourse of antiapartheid struggle in the 1980s and 1990s into a brand (a superstructuralism) promoting the "new" liberated and democratic South Africa, where the image of Mandela has been now copyrighted, costed, and protected from opportunistic and unauthorized commercial, ideological, and trademark appropriation.

The curse of poststructural semiology also found expression in Salvador Dali's seizure of the moment(s) of his dying to extend this "event" into a sign to communicate the uselessness of life and the ugliness of death. Dali thus transubstantiated himself into a sign that negated all other signs, including his own creations. Brian Rotman (1987) even tries to show that *nothing* signifies as a sign in its own right. Alternatively, Calvin Pryluck (1982) states rather than asks, "When is a sign not a sign?" Neither Barthes nor Dali could exist, even die, beyond semiology. Peirce held that "man" is himself a sign born into a universe "composed exclusively of signs," thus anticipating the dimension of the hyperreal ushered in by new media of the electrical, electronic, and virtual ages. Barthes and Dali themselves had become well-known signs through their iconic celebrity status – hence the metaphor of a jail and the problem of the real. Nelson Mandela however escaped both the real and discursive jails, and like Dali and Barthes became a sign – a disembodied hyperreal brand – in his own right.

The role of semiotics in visual culture has been widely commented on, in particular by Norman Bryson, Michael Ann Holly, and Keith Moxey (1994) and Jessica Evans and Stuart Hall (1999). Since their comments raise some crucial but not always sufficiently clarified points, they will be discussed in a little more detail here. Semiotics is the study of signs, both as integral systems and as modes of representation. Since iconic signs (those that resemble their object) are only one in a range of categories (which includes indexical – or pointer – signs, and symbolic – or arbitrary – signs), there is no particular reason to privilege them, as for example, some traditions of literary and art history have done. Visual culture's embrace of semiotics thus inevitably leads, as Bryson et al. has pointed out, to "art history's allegiance to an account of artistic creation that is based on the concept of resemblance or mimesis" being broken. The "richly textured semiotic discourse of the image" (Bryson et al. 1994: xviii) becomes thus the focus of interest, in particular in its interaction with the complex intertextual and intersemiotic components that constitute any cultural tradition.

A similarly comprehensive agenda for visual culture is set by Jessica Evans, who in the introduction to *Visual Culture: The Reader* (1999) says that:

> cultural studies rests on the achievements of semiotics as a whole and stakes its distinctiveness upon the analysis of the symbolic, classificatory and . . . meaning-making practices that are at the heart of all cultural production and consumption. Any study of the image conducted under the impact of cultural studies is indebted to semiotics. (1999: 3)

But Evans's rather simplified understanding of semiotics leads her unduly to limit its scope both as a critical and an exploratory device in visual culture. For semiotics is not only (as she seems to imply) hermeneutics but also semiology (as pointed out by Foucault [1966]). Semiotics is not just about the "meaning of any image or corpus of images" but about the way images are constructed and work within systems; it is also about the way they are interpreted, so what Evans sees as visual culture writers' concern with "a culture in which reproducibility provides the conditions of existence of any particular meaning" (1999: 3) is itself necessarily part of the semiological aspect of semiotics. Also her point about the importance of subjectivity in visual culture would have benefited from reference to the interpretant as understood in Peirce's semiotic. So when Evans suggests that subjectivity relativizes semiotics, it seems that she misunderstands the latter's scope. She writes:

> Part III, "Looking at Subjectivity," relativizes semiotics by shifting the emphasis away from the texts of representation to the question of the subject who is at the centre of meaning, but for whom meaning very often works below the threshold of consciousness. Here, our selection indicates that meaning is constituted not in the visual sign itself as a self-sufficient entity, nor exclusively in sociological positions and identities of the audience, but in the articulation between viewer and viewed, between the power of the image to signify and the viewer's capacity to interpret meaning. (1999: 4)

All this is of course precisely what Peircian semiotics set out to address with its careful elaboration of a series of interpretative strategies and associated analytical categories. An example of their usefulness in this respect can be seen in Chapter 6 of this volume in its Peircian semiotic analysis of the visual allegory of Britannia.

Ian Heywood and Barry Sandywell similarly present a somewhat over-simplified notion of the scope of semiotics in the realm of visual studies in their book *Interpreting Visual Culture* (1999). Although they affirm an understanding of hermeneutics as being "an *analytic* attitude towards the field of experience in which visual experience, is approached as a *socio-historical realm of interpretative practices*" (1999: xi; italics in original), they go on to say that they "have no intention of reducing these complexities to a grid of stable positions or set of general principles – along the lines of traditional semiotic or text-based critical theories" (1999: xi). Perhaps by "traditional semiotics" they mean the Saussure-based linguistic model that brackets the referent and is most concerned with the internal dyadic structure of the sign (as signifier and signified). However, on the other hand, the Peircian conception of semiotics, with its triadic emphasis on the complexity of the meaning-making process or *semiosis* on the part of the receiver, offers a range of categories that enable the specialist in visual culture, as in cultural studies, precisely to bring into focus the shifting impulses that characterize the interpretative process.

The triadic interrelation of significance in Peircian semiotics enables theorists to begin moving away from the dichotomies that seem to dog the ways of thinking that Europeans have tended to promote in the world over the last four centuries (if not longer). Debates have tended to follow agendas that have been set up in terms of these antithetical pairs of value ideas. By a process of force, stealth, habituation, and/or rhetorical naturalization, we have often accepted willy-nilly that these agendas are the only valid ones. Even writers like Ngugi Wa Thiong'O (1986), in drawing attention to the nature of Africa's historical condition, often describe it in the same terms that were used to colonize their antecedents. Common dualisms like good/evil, savagery/civilization, capitalism/socialism, superstition/progress, base/superstructure, and so on are liberally sprinkled throughout the literature of resistance in Africa. This is not the place to argue in any detail for the historical origins of the practice that generated this way of dividing up reality, but (even) European philosophers such as Jacques Derrida (1967) and Agnes Heller (1984) have suggested plausibly that this practice has been in use for as long as 2,500 years in one form or another.

The nature of the sign in Peirce is such that we can relate social entities – be they individual or collective – to discourse on the one hand and to practice on the other, in a quite coherent way. Since the semiotic relationship is triadic, a given situation can be analyzed in considerably more complex and creative ways than can be done via an application of a dyadic semiology alone. One has the means to look at the simultaneous relations between, for example, a sign and the habit it engenders in practice, the practice and the signifying subject, and the subject and the system of signification. It follows that any political aspects of such a situation cannot readily be separated out from such a study: one would first have to justify why any links cannot be hierarchical, and consequently *not* be political. Even if one interrelation within a triad is not necessarily definable in terms of superordination and subordination, it does not follow that either or both of the other links in the triad cannot so be defined (Tomaselli and Shepperson 1992).

Heywood and Sandywell are correct to stress the importance within the framework of visual culture of challenging the dominant Western concept of visual experience as *spectacle*, and to draw our attention to the persuasive rhetoric of visual representation that has traditionally influenced accounts of human experience.

The importance of intertextuality and intersemiotic reference to visual culture and to cultural studies is also worth stressing. Irit Rogoff affirms that "visual culture opens up an entire world of intertextuality in which images, sounds and spatial delineation are read on to and through one another" (quoted in Mirzoeff 2002: 24), and the notion of the intersemiotic – that is, the intermedial nature of this intertextuality – is no less potent a field for study within visual culture. For, as Rogoff suggests, visual culture proposes a "field of vision version of Derrida's concept of *différance*" in which "visual culture provides the visual articulation of the continuous displacement of the meaning in the field of vision and the visible" (2002: 25). The centrality of the concept of *spectacle* (as in Guy Debord's *La Société du spectacle* [1967]) in turn leads Nicholas Mirzoeff to emphasize the problematics of spectatorship within the visual world. "Spectatorship as an investigative field understands that what the eye purportedly 'sees' is dictated to it by an entire set of beliefs and desires and by a set of coded languages and generic apparatuses" (2002: 32). Here again Peircian categories relating to the interpretant and what Peirce calls "unlimited semiosis" (the continuous generation of new meaning via strings of interpretants generating new interpretants) provide valuable tools of analysis. Mirzoeff is also astute in his recognition of the importance to visual culture of reading space:

> To some extent the project of visual culture has been to try and repopulate space with all the obstacles and all the unknown images which the illusion of transparency evacuated from it. Space, as we have understood, is always differentiated: it is always sexual or racial; it is always constituted out of circulating capital; and it is always subject to the invisible boundary lines that determine inclusions and exclusions. (2002: 32)

This last comment of Mirzoeff clearly signals the anthropological or, more specifically, ethnological orientation of visual culture as a study area. For visual culture, in relativizing the productive but at the same time limiting grids applied by Renaissance art to visual experience and its analysis, implies an approach to the study of the latter that is at the same time both more comprehensive and more critical than that offered by traditional art history per se. As Foucault persuasively argues in *Les Mots et les choses*, human knowledge as acquired by each ethnic group, or by each distinctive period in the history of each group, tends to be the function of an often unconscious grid imposed on the chaos and multiplicity of experience, one that constitutes an *épistémè* or epistemological code. Since each *épistémè* implies both a semiology and a hermeneutics, it is as important to examine the codes governing each grid's construction (the *semiological* aspect) as well as the possibilities of meanings opened up (the *hermeneutic* aspect). In effect, ethnography is the study of the *épistémè* of a given society or ethnic group, and correspondingly concerns itself with as great a part as possible of the network of interrelations operative within it, a network in which, in theory, all signs are, by definition, to a greater or lesser extent significant. In this, ethnology provides an invaluable model and challenge to cultural studies as well as to visual culture.

While this volume does not systematically examine the role of ordinary interpreters (other than that provided implicitly by the authors of the chapters that follow), the way interpretants work via what Peirce calls "sign communities" would surely constitute a major part of a parallel study. Here, the authors rather discuss the ways in which general interpretations at different times emerge in response to historical conditions during specific epochs, and how these change over time. They offer more of a "structure of feeling" in the sense discussed by Raymond Williams (1979) – the mood of a period, the way people "feel" about their times and their relation to it. This feeling is inferred from a variety of sources – written, documents, photographic, musical, design, architecture, and so on.

We now turn specifically to the case studies and how they fit into the above general overview.

Semiotics: The Icon as Sign?

Icon is a term used nowadays in journalism and popular speech to signify a celebrity or cult object. *Icon*, in this sense, encodes the person or object so identified as personifying the exemplar of a particular generation, a stylistic epoch, and a feeling about a particular set of social experiences. Although the icon or cult object so identified is something with which we can all identify, it is at the same time a construction, a product deriving from the media, entertainment, or public relations industries. Although its origin is in the real, the operations to which it is submitted in the iconizing process transform it into a simulacrum. Madonna, the pop singer, for example, appropriates the status of the icons of early Christian religion, the Madonna who is the subject of medieval painting. She meshes this with other images and styles, past or contemporary, mythical or real, to create and live an image in which everything is fundamentally commodified and sexualized via performance. Madonna as mere woman disappears beneath the various guises that constitute her as an icon. The Madonna as an original medieval icon, on the other hand, being a sacred object, represented a real connection with its object. The religious belief invested in the Madonna enabled this figure as an icon to become attached to divinity. In the icons of today, the religious belief that enabled the icon to become virtually as one with its object is replaced by hypermediated representation that elevates an otherwise banal icon to celebrity status, one which often occludes the reality of the object it represents.

Broadly speaking, cultural icons may be seen to work in three different ways: first, as true icons invested with religious significance; second, as secular icons, objects, or persons in the real world that through time accrue to themselves a certain exemplary cultural status; and third, as constructed icons, which in particular are those that in the twentieth century have been manufactured to sell a product, service, or an idea. With the progressive desacralization of the typical medieval icon, the iconic sign becomes separated from its object. The sign becomes a simulacrum that substitutes – mediatizes – the original person or object into something else that becomes progressively susceptible to commercial exploitation. The image of Nelson Mandela is now regularly appropriated and branded to market, among other things, South Africa and AIDS prevention, while the Eiffel Tower stands for Paris and the Little Mermaid promotes tourism to Copenhagen. The chapters that follow either explicitly or implicitly apply the method of semiotics to examine this process of iconization.

In specifically semiotic terms, icons are signs that resemble their objects whether their object is a thing in the real world, an idea, or another sign. They also of course include indexical and symbolic functions in that they point to their objects and often become conventional signs. Although this imitative quality might in fact lead one to believe that the icon comes closest to its object, this is, in fact, often not the case. Icons can be deceitful to the extent that they occlude as much as represent their object. The Holy Lance is one such perverse, deceitful sign: a heroic myth born thousands of years ago, but which has since been appropriated by neo-Nazis.

An index draws attention to something else, the unseen; it is where denotation and connotation reside. The Eiffel Tower once denoted the power of mechanization but now connotes meanings that have nothing to do with this original quality. The index always points to its object and is always in a relation of contiguity with it: the interpretant of the index may not always deduce what the indicated object is, but this is not the fault of the index in its dynamic function. The interpretant is the idea to which a sign gives rise, linked in associational chains of signification where meanings roll into one another, constantly reshaping interpretations, via the process of unlimited semiosis. It is at this second level that Barthes's concept of myth is located. Myth, in the semiotic sense, naturalizes meaning, suggesting that it has always been so, timeless. In the chapter on Mandela, for example, the media and popular myth of Mandela is deconstructed to reveal that the genesis of the Mandela myth is far more complex and contradictory than is commonly assumed.

The symbol, being a conventional sign, and often arbitrary in its form of relation to its object, does not pretend in normal circumstances to be contiguous with, or imitative of that to which it refers. Through the symbol, icons and indexes combine into narratives, ways of making sense, and sometimes into grand narratives. The Eiffel Tower, once standing for industrial development and the centennial commemoration of the French Revolution, has long since become disarticulated from these original meanings, and is now an open symbolic sign representing aspects of Paris: tourism, romance, innovation.

Symbols are part of a conventional system of representation and the interpretant must be familiar with this system to interpret any sign within it. The icon, on the other hand, though seeming to imitate its object, often operates as much or more on the level of symbol or index. In this way the gap between icon and object can be filled with *invisible* layers of semiotic function that, like successive glazes or laminates of glass, both highlight and occlude the object.

Cultural icons are iconic signs to which a transparent but often complex overlayering of connotations has accrued, usually after a certain period of time. Where celebrities are concerned the connotations are deliberate, manufactured, relentless, and take on their significance via intensive marketing and public relations. They eventually come to work at the level of myth where these carefully manufactured connotations become discursively hegemonic. In the case of an icon, Madonna for example, they take on an almost religious dimension, as fans confer ontological significance on the image. The icons discussed in this book are, however, of a kind different from those normally described in semiotic textbooks. In this use, the icon is a first order sign, operating primarily at the level of appearance. In this role it exists in and of itself, but begins to take on additional meanings when it interacts with the second and third orders of index and symbol respectively. The longer the history of the icon, the richer the layering of indexical and symbolic significances organically attached to it, though some more recent or contemporary icons (such as Marilyn Monroe or Nelson Mandela) also manage in a relatively short period of time to achieve this status. In this common sense use, the icon is simultaneously icon (appearance), indexical (connota tive), and symbolic (explanatory). A British Airways magazine published in 1993, for example, writes about "The Power of Brand Mandela." This kind of "branding" is usually made possible by the intense iconization/ mediatization (especially through cinema and television) of the icon that, through its mass audience and instantaneous dissemination, can rapidly propel an image or object to iconic status. This status retains the appearance of the object and simultaneously encodes qualities not necessarily intrinsic to it. Hence the invention of the term *iconization*.

Iconization eliminates contradiction, celebrates the unity of surface appearance, and denies history. It occurs in the continuous present, so that icons can be appropriated to many kinds of discursive (re-)engineering.

It is also the aim of the essays collected in this volume to analyze the way cultural icons – objects, living or mythical personalities – are constructed and disseminated, and to assess the implications, in semiotic and cultural terms, of the exceptional accretion of meaning and popular recognition attached to them. In doing this the volume explores a classic range of iconic forms – paintings (Edvard Munch's *The Scream*), national symbols (Britannia), monuments (the Eiffel Tower, the Little Mermaid), artifacts (the Holy Lance), and living figures (Nelson Mandela and Steve Biko).

To properly understand the exponential accretion of meaning in visual icons, and more particularly cultural icons, it is useful to situate the phenomenon in the wider field of contemporary culture in particular, insofar as it has become a predominantly visual one. For the modern and postmodern worlds represent above all a culture of the icon. A visual culture is one in which signs and meanings are primarily a function of visual apprehension. Such a culture dates back in Europe to the Renaissance, which marked an important break with the pre-Gutenberg audile-tactile culture as analyzed by Marshall McLuhan (1962). In the medieval world, the aural, oral, and tactile were closely bound up with the visual. Post-Renaissance culture witnessed an increasing separation of the senses in a quest for knowledge and in cultural experience. With the empirical model of science, based on close observation, and the spatialization of knowledge's recording and dissemination (aided by print technology and post-Renaissance painting techniques), European culture became increasingly visual in its orientation. Despite the resurgence of the audile-tactile in the modern media and electronic age, the visual remains the predominant mode of cultural apprehension and expression. This is reflected in the (post-) modern world's obsession with visual icons. It is a world in which the visual sign can more readily lose the cautions that parallel or complementary modes of perception and representation (hearing/sound; touch/texture; smell/flavor) would traditionally have applied to it. It is the seduction of the image itself, in its color and form, that becomes the central focus of attention.

Visual icons become cultural icons when they take on functions that transcend the immediate or intended role or purpose of the object or sign on which they are based. They do this in a number of ways, most or all of which need to be present for the visual sign to attain to cultural iconic status:

- by accreting layers of meaning or connotation
- by representing continuity
- by multiplying their representative function
- by attaining an exemplary status
- by attracting intense mediatization, very often through various patterns of intermedial transformation
- by exerting a certain seduction

The relation between these functions and the way they accrue is more or less cumulative and successive. The first requirement, then, is for the icon to be susceptible to the accretion of layers of meaning or connotation. We see this process operative in the construction of national icons such as Britannia, in the gradual expansion of the range of connotations attached to the Eiffel Tower, and in the heightening of the significance of a personality such as Nelson Mandela, not only as man and an individual destiny, but also as a figurehead and national, racial, or ideological representative. Very often, specific connotations or significances attached to cultural icons are contradictory, but for the icon to endure, these contradictions must become subsumed into a dialectical dynamic that is capable of accommodating shifts and reversals of meaning. Such patterns are well brought out in the chapter on the Eiffel Tower. Munch's painting, *The Scream,* is described by the Munch Museum catalogue in decidedly innocent and unthreatening terms, while the painting's subsequent iconization has led to its use to indicate anxiety, fear, and madness. The ultimate madness and anxiety was perhaps shown in its theft from the museum, which will add a new layer of signification to it.

For a visual sign to attain cultural iconic status it is also necessary that it should represent continuity within a culture and survive historical change. This aspect of the cultural icon is elucidated in particular in the chapter on Nelson Mandela, a living sign, whose iconic status is thus far from being fixed. In this way his figure offers the opportunity to investigate the complexities, paradoxes, and occasional contradictions of the cultural icon, seized as it were almost in the very process of their actualization. The role of the media in this process in the late twentieth-century world is of course a most important one; in particular in the way it can disarticulate original meanings and rearticulate them into new meanings that may have little relation to the originals.

The multiplication of the cultural icon's representative function is of course both a continuation and transformation of the accretion to them of multiple connotations. Once again this presents us with a paradox: a cultural icon must be both fixed (that is, recognizable, representing continuity) and mobile (open to the imposition of new layers of meaning or identity). Often this shift, as it were, to a higher level or representative status within a culture is the result of intermedial transformation. So, for example, the tale of the Little Mermaid that finds its exemplary textual expression in Hans Christian Anderson only attains iconic status when reiconized as a piece of sculpture and placed in a significant cultural context (the approach to the Danish capital, Copenhagen). More generally, the promotion to representative function involves the opening of the icon to identification at a high level of popular recognition: a city, a state, a country, a national or spiritual movement. Not all such cultural promotions are of course necessarily salutary. So the progressive misuse or perversion of a relic as highly charged as the Holy Lance in the Vienna is enthrallingly investigated in one chapter of this book.

The attainment by the visual icon of an exemplary status implies a certain moral as well as semiotic power, one that enables the sign to express *values* as well as more secular meanings. So the Little Mermaid, Steve Biko, Nelson Mandela, and Britannia as icons all have powerful moral resonance. And even such problematic images as Munch's *The Scream* or the Holy Lance are shown in their respective chapters to owe much of their power to the ambiguous moral messages they contain. More generally the exemplary status of cultural icons is also a function of a certain aesthetic regularity, one that is often as much a function of medial glamorization or intermedial transformation.

Susceptibility to mediatization, whether through cinematographic, televisual, or other kinds of medial dissemination, is a particularly vital component of the cultural icon in the modern age. Of course, the cultural icon, even in its earlier historical forms, has always depended on medial presentation for its establishment in the popular consciousness. What has changed today is merely the rate at which such mediatization occurs and the ambiguities instituted by the different forms of representation to which the icon is submitted. Once again, a contemporary figure such as Nelson Mandela provides an opportunity to investigate some of the issues at stake in this process.

Finally, for cultural icons to establish themselves with any power, they must be seductive. In other words, they must be able to maintain a broad appeal to their public, while lending themselves to transformation and development. Originally, this appeal would have been religious. In a secular or early modern age the seductive imperative was moral or social. In the postmodern age it is becoming intensely sensual and sexual. In all these stages, nevertheless, aesthetics played an important part, in particular in its consecration of icons through representation as works of art or through the various media. But the aesthetic aspect also signals the potentially factitious and deceitful face of the cultural icon. Like icons in general, cultural icons purport to represent their object, but as this book will show, in many cases this representation can be highly problematic. Not least of the challenges cultural icons offer to the modern cultural commentator, therefore, is that of critical investigation or deconstruction necessary to investigate their moral and aesthetic ambiguity.

References

Alpers, S. (1996). Visual Culture Questionnaire. *October* 77.

Arnold, M. (1966). *Culture and Anarchy*. Cambridge: Cambridge University Press.

Bal, M., ed. (1999). *The Practice of Cultural Analysis: Exposing Interdisciplinary Interpretation*. Stanford, CA: Stanford University Press.

Barthes, R. (1974). *S/Z: An Essay*. New York: Hill and Wang.

Baudrillard, J. (1970). *La Société de consommation*. Paris: Denoël.

———. (1972). *Pour une critique de l'économie politique du signe*. Paris: Gallimard.

———. (1976). *L'Echange symbolique et la mort*. Paris: Gallimard.

———. (1981). *Simulacres et simulation*. Paris: Galilée.

Blonsky, M., ed. (1985). *On Signs*. Oxford: Blackwell.

Bryson, N., M. A. Holly, and K. Moxey, eds. (1994). *Images and Visual Culture: Interpretations*. Hanover, NH and London: Wesleyan University Press.

Debord, G. (1992). *La Société du spectacle*. Paris: Gallimard. (Orig. pub. date 1967.)

Derrida, J. (1967). *De la Grammatologie*. Paris: Minuit.

During, S., ed. (1999). *The Cultural Studies Reader*. London: Routledge. (Orig. pub. date 1993.)

Evans, J. and S. Hall, eds. (1999). *Visual Culture: The Reader*. London: Sage.

Foster, H. (1996). *The Return of the Real: The Avant-garde at the End of the Century*. Boston: MIT Press.

Foucault, M. (1966). *Les Mots et les choses. Une archéologie des sciences humaines*. Paris: Gallimard.

Heller, A. (1984). *A Radical Philosophy*. Oxford: Basil Blackwell.

Heywood, I. and B. Sandywell, eds. (1999). *Interpreting Visual Culture: Explorations in the Hermeneutics of the Visual*. London: Routledge.

Husserl, E. (1969). *Ideas Pertaining to a General Introduction to Pure Phenomenology*. London: Allen and Unwin.

Jameson, F. (1972). *The Prison House of Language*. Princeton, NJ: Princeton University Press.

McLuhan, M. (1962). *The Gutenberg Galaxy*. London: Routledge.

Mirzoeff, N., ed. (2002, first ed. 1998). *The Visual Culture Reader*. London: Routledge.

Peirce, C. S. (1966). *Collected Papers* (vols. 7 and 8, ed. Arthur W. Burks). Cambridge, MA: Harvard University Press. See in particular vol. 8, ch. 5, On Signs, 210–13; ch. 8, To Lady Welby. On Signs and the Categories, 220–31; On the Classification of Signs, 231–45.

Pryluck, C. (1982). Cuando un Signo no es Signo. *Video-Forum* 14, 127–37.

Rotman, B. (1987). *Signifying Zero: The Semiotics of Nothing*. London: Macmillan.

Saussure, F. de (1972). *Cours de linguistique générale*. Paris: Payot.

Tomaselli, K. G. and A. Shepperson. (1992). Popularising Semiotics. *Communication Research Trends* 11(1).

Tylor, E. B. (1924). *Primitive Culture*. New York: Brentano's.

wa Thiong'o, N. (1986). *Petals of Blood*. Oxford: Heinemann International Literature and Textbooks.

Williams, R. (1979). *Politics and Letters; Interviews with New Left Review*. London: New Left Books.

THE ABSENT SIGNIFIER:
THE MORPHING OF NELSON MANDELA

Keyan G. Tomaselli and Arnold Shepperson

It is pretty much common cause that Nelson Mandela – former political prisoner, state president, and later, continental peacemaker – was one of the most outstanding media figures of the final decades of the twentieth century. Certainly, one could make the case that he was, alongside the likes of Mohandas K. Gandhi, Albert Einstein, Albert Schweitzer, and Winston Churchill, one of the most representative figures of what the popular media held to be the "best" of the time.

During apartheid (1948–1990) activists referred to "the idea of Mandela" or the "ideas" for which Steve Biko stood. Encoded in this use of the word *idea* are complex, abstract political concepts arising directly out of the history of the antiapartheid struggle. While supporters of Biko and Mandela in South Africa had at least an intuitive understanding of the content of the "idea" associated with these two figures, for American audiences, these ideas were reduced to one personality within the social realm in which they are principal actors (Tomaselli and Boster 1993).

The American civil rights movement, for example, is personified in Martin Luther King, Jr.; glasnost and perestroika were reported as being all Gorbachev's doing. These kinds of reductionisms keep the issues simple enough for people to understand without the need for deeper analysis. But the problem is that these media-constructed personalities begin to hide the complex political processes they personify. They are then framed by the media into opposing symbols: the Cuban missile crisis, for instance, was reported as a conflict between Kennedy and Khrushchev, and in South

Africa, it was Mandela against first, P. W. Botha, and then later a reconstructed "Other," F. W. de Klerk, who was later to release him.

Our analysis will examine, via the Phaneroscopic Table (Table 1.1), the way that Mandela was constructed by the US media in particular. This articulation is designed to offer an understanding of South Africa articulated via US history. The civil rights discourses applied to position Mandela vis-à-vis the South African struggle, as we shall show, largely resulted in the myth of Steve Biko being incorporated into the myth of Mandela, who could not be understood without his alter ego, De Klerk.

Structuring Absence: The Man with No Face

In general cultural terms, an individual is nurtured by her or his community through a communal learning experience. Whatever is new for an individual child is something that: a) has all been done before for the oldest generation present, and b) is some form of labor for the generation in between (Shepperson 1995: 55). For any emerging generation, cultural signs are *as such* emotionally received. For white South Africans, Nelson Mandela while in prison was a demonic, communist antihero. For blacks, in contrast, he was a positive democratic hero, a political martyr. The irony was that Mandela was a man with no face: pictures of him had been banned. Apart from one banned photograph taken prior to his arrest in 1962, no one knew what he looked like.

When some significant sign-artifact or image takes on the status of what is commonly called a "cultural icon," those who declare this sign's status are in effect setting out a specific interpretation of their own reception of their condition. Decisively, however, this interpretation is made concrete not for the original generation of founders, *but for generations still to come*. This chapter will examine how Mandela was visually and ideologically morphed or iconicized from an invisible communist, a deceitful sign, to that of an proactive capitalist; from antihero to superhero; and from an abstract, "invisible" idea to a concrete, visible icon.

It is a tautology that future generations cannot *experience* the present. Because of this, cultural icons have to embody some aspect of the founding generation's present in ways that engender a special kind of recognition in its successor generations. If we look beyond the essentially static analysis of significance inherent in the signifier-signified sign relation, and incorporate the essentially incarnate nature of a generation of signifying communities that might *want* to be seen as culturally coherent, then cultural icons *and the activities associated therewith* become the basic unit of analysis. For a future generation, public activities involving iconic figures or images like Mandela will be a focus around which younger generations will be expected to develop specific attachments (emotional interpretants)

Table 1.1 The phaneroscopic table.

Orders of signification	Phaneroscopy	2nd trichotomy of signs		Nature of semiotic interaction	Phenomenology
1	Firstness: Central idea	Icon		Encounter	Being-three
2	Secondness: Identity in the face of the other	Index:	Denotation Connotation Myth	Experience Transmission/transmitted texts	Activity/doing Reading/writing Conceived/received texts
3	Thirdness: Codes/syntagma Modes of relations	Symbol:	Myth Commonsense Ideology	Intelligibility making sense	Public signs

in respect to their identity beyond the family. How is it that Mandela's ideological rehabilitation was achieved by the world's media; how did they positively animate him – and rehabilitate the ideas he stood for – from a condition of suspended iconic determination while he was in prison to one of a proactive problem solver, a national asset as enduring (but much shorter lived) than, for example, Britannia? Where Britannia is an abstract idea, Mandela after 1990 became more than a mere quality, a man with a face, a personality and a mission – but a face struggled over and competed for across the world. One article even tried to estimate the financial value of the Mandela brand! (Sampson 2003: 22)

We follow fairly strictly Charles Peirce's conception of iconicity in discussing the general term *cultural icon*. Using a similar pragmatic imperative, we derive a way of conceiving the term *culture* based on elements of Raymond Williams's early writing on the topic. Thereafter, we will apply this analysis to a theoretical treatment of a selection of instances in which the figure, name, or presence of Nelson Mandela was particularly prominent. Keeping with Peirce's general concept of the sign as the basic building block of logic, we will distinguish ways in which the use of Mandela as a sign could be seen as either a symbol or index generated from other icons, or where it acted in a genuinely iconic manner in its own right. We will discuss these instances in the light of semiotics as a normative science that presupposes a prior ethics and aesthetics, in relation to how these norms apply to the agents and objects of culture.

The Continuity of Cultural Experience

In the present historical phase of contested modernity, other sets of symbols (words, objects, visual signs, ritual actions, etc.) that assist an individual or group in meeting the ultimate problems of identity and destiny have replaced confessional religion as the central signifying practice in contemporary society. This *civil religion* denotes the ritual dimension of the state. As such, it is associated with both the exercise of power and the constant regeneration of the social order. This remnant of the premodern religious-political form of life continues to act as a form of transcendent justification for social and cultural action (Moodie 1975: 295–98). However, Moodie tends to speak of this civil religion as a "symbolic universe, within the boundaries of which articulation may take place for a body politic, however defined" (1975: 298). We will deviate from this, however, to argue that in this context the aesthetic employment of iconic figures or images is actually the prerequisite for civil-religious forms of ritual. This permits the conception of a cultural icon to maintain a line of continuity with the earlier conception of a religious icon – which accords with the transformation from devil to the status of superhero that Mandela attained in the 1990s. This image, as we argue below, is a composite of a number of well-known actors and activist personalities through which the media reconstructed the earlier "man with no face."

The use of the cultural icon generally involves highly public ritual displays, many of which are intended to involve whole families and communities. The eldest generation present embodies some already-determined or symbolic aspect of community life. Mandela was not easily rehabilitated for the white generation, which, during apartheid, largely approved of his being incarcerated. The middle generation serves to demonstrate the working of this aspect indexically. Many white activists and liberals understood Mandela in the 1980s to be an indicator of hope, of a political solution with regard to a racially traumatized society at war with itself. In turn, the youngest generation absorbs the emotional signals that present these continuities iconically as the unities and identities they will come to enact and embody in due course. Tomaselli's two children, at age ten and twelve, for example, were beside themselves with excitement at meeting Mandela in 1994 at a Natal University graduation ceremony, where Mandela was being conferred an honorary doctorate (and their mother, a PhD). The children's image of Mandela was mainly built by watching Mandela's release on TV (in the US where they were living at the time) and via their friendship with the children of Mandela's personal financial advisor, their neighbors. The direction of these ritual activities at the youngest generation present represents a clear relation between meaning and emotion (aesthesis), a connection found explicitly in Peirce (Shepperson 1995: 59). Significantly, the children declared Mandela to be "boring" following his long, politically turgid speech in which the exciting image of the man personally known to the neighbors was vitiated by an address directed, not at children, but at the graduates. The chasm between the myth and the reality, however, did not dent their support for the man who brought peace and hope to the land.

The use of iconic images or figures is a maneuver that endows continuity on some aspect of the identity of a given human group or aggregation. This comes about precisely in the sense that iconicity in both the semiotic and religious senses is the condition under which a sign has a quality of sameness in its actual presence as a sign, which largely remains over time irrespective of the interpretations assigned to it under any given set of conditions. Thus the presence of the sign, whether visual or auditory or even olfactory, must become (or, as we show below, be made to become) familiar across the three generations of an identifiable group or aggregation for it to have cultural status. This certainly did occur in the case of Mandela, though with different inflections. There are consequently two factors that relate to the conception of continuity under these circumstances: (1) in semiotic terms, the icon is the element of the sign that guarantees its continuity prior to any contingent meanings (Ransdell 1997: 39–41); and (2) historically, "culture' as a political conception is associated with the continuity of human social, political, and linguistic aggregations (Williams 1965: 67).

In terms of the continuity of icons, Peirce's later thinking (see Ransdell 1997) was driven by his recognition that the heterogeneity of the universe was both a result of evolutionary developments (we evolve "by force of habit" [Peirce, vol. 6, 1965–66: 300]), and as a result of some element of continuity that links the plurality of reality. The antagonistic ideas for which Mandela originally stood for in different constituencies and generations, for example, were remade into a set of compatible ideas like "democracy," "reconciliation," and "peace." It is the iconicity of signs that endows them with a continuity in time with previous manifestations of the sign. The fact that Mandela as a visual icon was previously unknown provided the opportunity for the media to reengineer his public image even before it was known what he looked like as an old man. As a structured absence in the apartheid era, Mandela and the African National Congress (ANC) were faced on his release on 11 February 1990 with the task of making manifest the man himself. The question was, would he live up to the myth created for him by the international media and his constituency? Semiotics, and therefore iconicity, thus presupposes an ethics and an aesthetics.

In the case of cultural icons, we have a situation in which we qualify as "cultural" the following: (1) a quality of being admirable associated with some object; (2) acts of will that are continuous with the admirableness of (1), and which as such constitute the conduct of these acts of will as "right"; and (3) an aspect of significance in this admirability that maps onto other objects in some exemplary fashion defined in terms of (1) and (2). These criteria in effect derive from the relation between sign and object in Peirce's three-way sign relation where a signs stands *to* its object *for* an interpretant. Where a sign in standing to its object *functions towards* or *maps onto* its object(s), the same sign operates on its interpretant to create an effect that necessarily takes the form of a habit.

Now if an icon, as effectively the *tone* or *quality of continuity* of a sign, is to qualify in some or other cultural sense, then the term *cultural icon* must be proper to some class of sign relations that operates on those habits (as *interpretants*) we consider to be cultural. Mandela came to signify the general idea of a unified, nonracial South Africa – a country that prior to 1994 had never been unified, nonracial, nor even a nation. Mandela's face (icon) was used by all manner of parastatal companies to advertise their products and services, for example, South African Airways. Mandela thus was understood to be above party politics, and therefore, as superhero he was never tainted by politics – he was as pure and innocent as Britannia (see Scott, in this volume). Culturally, too, Mandela the superhero offered a panacea, a way through barbarism and paganistic, communist-led destruction. He offered redemption, forgiveness, and exorcism. In this guise, Mandela's role was not that dissimilar to Raymond Williams's discussion of culture.

Principally, Williams (1958) saw the concept of culture as emerging in two distinct (and distinctly English) approaches to overcoming the disruptions associated with the Industrial Revolution: Some followed a development of the medievalist tradition and saw culture as a kind of "redemptive" solution to the divisive class politics of industrialization. Others proposed that the attainment of culture serve as a qualification for (usually) the working classes' admission into the broader ranks of English society.

In each case, the term should be understood, pragmatically speaking, as taking *culture* to indicate those accomplished tasks of inhabiting, looking after, and so on, that mark the quality of how an individual or class aggregation bears the results of *having been* looked after in a place. Reading Williams thus, we could say that a person exhibits culture in the sense that one has absorbed those habits that mark one as a member of the aggregation called "English." Mandela performed this function for South Africa. Returning expatriate white South Africans to the country after 1994 were astonished at the (new) flag-waving populace, one where the flag adorns any and every kind of artifact, from the houses of parliament to condoms on AIDS posters plastered everywhere. Culture, put simply, then, is that ensemble of iconic qualities the accomplishment of which establishes a new generation as members of a continuously developing human aggregation. The new flag had been one of the conveyers (or sign vehicles) for this aggregation, while Mandela was seen to be its "author." It is the quality of how an aggregation's existing generations have accomplished to date the business of developing new generations' endowments into talents that reproduce the aggregation as a recognizable unitary community into an indefinite future. Mandela forged an (if fragile and contested) imagined community against all odds. We now apply this theory to an analysis of Mandela as a cultural icon at the turn of the third millennium.

Icons in Action: Nelson Mandela in the Mass Media (1987–1990)

In this section we will examine three instances in which the name, figure, and image of Mandela took an especially prominent place in the mass media. The occasions under review are:

1. the release of the Home Box Office (HBO) docu-drama miniseries *Mandela* in 1987, starring Danny Glover as Mandela;[1]

2. the *Freedom Fest* (11 June 1988) internationally broadcast pop festival and its follow-up *Tribute for a Free South Africa* (16 April 1990);[2] and
3. the media feeding frenzy that occurred with Mandela's release from Pollsmoor Prison in February 1990.[3]

We will argue that although Mandela was presented as an icon in himself, there are ways of seeing his appearance in these instances as predominantly symbolic or indexical, with other images in fact serving as marks or qualities of continuity for the producers of the images. The HBO docudrama, *Mandela* (1987), was a 120-minute miniseries, the release of which in the US and Britain in early 1990 coincided with the making of the myth of Mandela as a worthy successor to Steve Biko, immortalized in Richard Attenborough's *Cry Freedom* (1987). The miniseries takes the form of a superhero tale, presenting its subject as a larger-than life messiah, indomitable and powerful. The serial takes its characters and social dimensions straight out of a comic book, with heroes and villains defined to the point of caricature, and no hyperbole wasted when either Nelson or an apartheid-supporting National Party member speaks.

Immediately noticeable is Mandela's (Glover's) physical size in relation to his colleagues. Glover, also the star of two *Lethal Weapon* films, is a towering, broad figure who dominates the screen to the extent that, at the end of the scene, the other two actors must peer around him to edge into the frame at all. Glover's physical presence immediately minimizes the roles of brothers in arms Walter Sisulu and Oliver Tambo, while magnifying Mandela's. Another device used by the director is to dress the ANC leaders in a sort of uniform, consisting of nearly identical gray suits with black ties. The suits are corporate gear to the point of stereotyping, conferring on their wearers status and responsibility, prestige and respectability. For audiences in deeply conservative America, this appearance contradicted the idea of communist terrorists, with which the ANC was labeled by prominent conservatives such as Senator Jesse Helms. It also conceals the fact that it was the CIA who tipped off the South African police as to the whereabouts of Mandela, which resulted in his arrest, trial, and jail for twenty-seven years.

In the series's representation of Mandela's final trial, as the camera focuses on him, we see him wearing traditional African clothing for the first time. The rest of the ANC leaders seated behind him are all wearing grey suits. Clothing Glover differently in this courtroom scene serves a basic Hollywood precept: when possible, *make your star stand out*. This dress thus portrayed Mandela as a traditional African representing traditional (black) South Africans, with the other ANC members portrayed as a sort of cabinet. By this stage, Mandela's personal struggle has become the narrative focus, stressing the injustice of his imprisonment over that of the cause for which he had actually fought.

The original release of *Mandela* more or less simultaneously with Attenborough's *Cry Freedom* in 1987 placed the living figure of Mandela in a special relationship with American awareness of the South African antiapartheid tradition. While he was still alive, Steve Biko's political philosophy and program were only sporadically covered in the larger American newspapers. Following his death on 12 September 1977, however, the US media treated Biko as one of South Africa's most important black leaders (Brown 1980: 31). None of the previous nineteen deaths in detention had received anything like the saturation coverage Biko's death received. The martyrdom of Biko provided the foundation for the later emergence of Nelson Mandela as a folk hero in the US and British media. The dead symbol of resistance against apartheid was meshed with the living sign that was Mandela.

The morphing of Glover with Mandela occurred in the week prior to Mandela's release. Mandela was the cover story on *Time* of that early week in April 1990. Since no one at *Time*'s publisher knew what Mandela looked like, their sketch artist constructed an identikit of Mandela, which they claimed had been approved by Nelson's wife, Winnie. When discussing this in a media class at the University of North Carolina, Chapel Hill, William Sudderth drew a correspondence between Glover and *Time*'s identikit of Mandela, and suggested that this image was linked to the impending re-release of the TV series. As it turned out, Mandela the real man in no way looked like Glover the actor. The moment between De Klerk's announcement of the impending release of Mandela and the re-release of the TV series, both owned by Time-Warner, offered Time and HBO's marketers an iconic conjuncture during which an abstract idea (*of* Mandela) preceded any image of him (firstness). Having articulated Mandela (the identikit) in the image of Glover, *Time* thus merged the myth of Mandela with the myth played by Glover, to come up with a movie character rearticulated in terms of Hollywood imperatives and global capital. In other words, the *idea* of the sign (Mandela) – the absent signifier – is indexically articulated into an image based on Glover (secondness), and thereafter into a form of intelligibility (thirdness) that stands for the relational idea of black liberation and Western-style democracy. Other than the name of Mandela, which was known, the lack of a visual icon meant that the second trichotomy worked in reverse, from the symbol back to the icon, on his release. What was articulated and disarticulated were opposing central ideas – white, Western democratic ideals versus Soviet-inspired communism. We call this reverse semiosis *iconization*.

The *FreedomFest* and *Tribute* concerts' coincidentally also lie in the death of Biko, despite their focus on, respectively, the call for Mandela's release and the celebration thereof. Apartheid first entered the pop music lexicon with Peter Gabriel's "Biko" (from the *Melt* LP, 1980), followed in

1984 by Special AKA's "Free Nelson Mandela" (from their *In The Studio* LP). Both became cult classics in America, with Amnesty International using "Biko" for its tours, on its records, and during *FreedomFest* itself. Special AKA's record hit the British top ten, its catchy video, sharp lyrics, and danceable music confronting the issue of apartheid through rock music on a mass scale for the first time (Fisher 1989: 64).

Although pop music is largely unable to express complex or subtle ideas, many artists use a modern anthemic form to express political concepts. These anthems are usually aligned to either an individual within the issue (e.g., Biko or Mandela), or lowest-common-denominator themes within an issue, like boycotting Sun City, the gaudy casino entertainment complex in the then Bophuthatswana bantustan. Within the field of antiapartheid activism, it was common for people to speak of "the idea of Mandela" or the "ideas" for which Steve Biko stood. In this activist context the use of the word, *idea* covers complex, abstract political concepts; for American audiences, however, these ideas have been reduced to the individual personalities within the social realm in which they are principal actors.

The boundaries of the conflict are thus clearly drawn, defined as it were by the personalities of the antagonists. Under this mode of apprehension the Mandela/De Klerk couplet translates readily into a black vs. white conflict (see Fisher 1989: 1–2). So when the *FreedomFest* concert took place it meshed the above interpretations with two other crucial elements. First was the very close support, affection, and loyalty Mandela received during his imprisonment from his wife and his two daughters by her. This sense of family appealed to middle ground Britons and Americans who had been alienated by radical demands for sanctions against South Africa. Second, the remarkable length of Mandela's incarceration for "a philosophical crime" (Perryman 1998) ensured him an uncontested moral stature, positioning him as the prime architect of a future democratic South Africa. By connecting these ideas with a celebration of Mandela's seventieth birthday, the organizers of *FreedomFest* provided a spectacular media moment. *FreedomFest* effectively simplified apartheid, either following the anthemic pattern of the songs that highlighted the event, or through comparing the struggle in South Africa to the US civil rights movement. Stevie Wonder's on-stage statement is a good example of this appropriation of the South African struggle into civil rights discourse, adopting an identifiable strategic style through its tone and word choice. Yet the implied connection between the situations of African American and South African blacks did not and does not really exist.

With the *Tribute for a Free South Africa* concert, the organizers assumed that Mandela's personal appearance would clinch the US TV rights. But not a single US station signed up because of a lack of time to sell advertising space, and worries about "politics" (Dineslow 1989: 284). The event was, however, broadcast to forty-five other countries, twenty-one fewer than for the 1988 concert. Thus where the Fox Television Network had broadcast a full six hours of the *FreedomFest* event, American viewers had no direct coverage of the later *Tribute* concert. The presence of Mandela as a theme failed, therefore, to elicit any major media attention (apart from some fairly prominent coverage in the tabloid *USA Today*). To get some idea of how this shift may have come about, we will turn to the last of our three examples, the media bean-feast that accompanied Mandela's release from prison and its immediate aftermath.

Mandela's release from prison took place on 11 February 1990, about a week after the then state president, F. W. de Klerk, had announced the repeal of legislation banning organizations like the ANC and the South African Communist Party (SACP). During his announcement of the repeal, De Klerk had also given notice of Mandela's imminent release. Though the release had not been scheduled, because it was widely expected the world's media had plenty of time to put together a major campaign to cover the release of apartheid's most famous prisoner.

In the case of the US media, it was soon apparent that its anchormen had little grasp of the situation. In one instance, the *MacNeil/Lehrer NewsHour*'s Robin MacNeil simply ran out of questions, with the interviewee, South African Minister of Constitutional Affairs Gerrit Viljoen, having to explain to the interviewer just what the ANC stood for, and what the situation was about. When Dan Rather interviewed Mandela shortly after his release, his questions tended to concentrate on Mandela as a personality, revealing little to American viewers of the conditions and popular expectations that had influenced Mandela's response to the leadership role the media had attributed to him.

In reality Mandela's release, following as it did shortly after De Klerk's major parliamentary speech, proved to be more of a showcase for media personalities than it did for Mandela. Within days of De Klerk's announcement, Dan Rather and Tom Brokaw arrived in South Africa. Simon Barber, a veteran correspondent on the South African situation, remarked acerbically that they

> were on hand for their own glory and that of their networks, not because they had any special clue about the place that would enlighten their audiences. For them, South Africa was just one more stop on a travelling roadshow called Megahistory 1990 in which network anchormen hop around the globe to parade their faces in front of historic backdrops and get in the way of correspondents on the ground who may actually know something. (Tomaselli and Teer-Tomaselli 2003)

By dint of some adroit interviews that exploited the aura surrounding Mandela's release, the apartheid National Party government actually succeeded in generating quite sympathetic reporting from the US media. This certainly did them no harm as Mandela's freedom unleashed pent-up resentments in regions that had borne the brunt of apartheid policy, like the "independent republics" of Bophuthatswana, Transkei, and Ciskei. In effect, Mandela's release had the contradictory result that news from South Africa began to focus not only on the long and intricate "talks about talks" that ensued, but also on the still white-dominated state's efforts to deal with the frequently violent results of the unleashing of these resentments.

Previously, a casual glance could associate Mandela with the totality of black antiapartheid struggle. Mandela became America's media symbol of the black antiapartheid struggle just as Martin Luther King, Jr. was the personification of the civil rights movement. Various factors contributed to Mandela's popular appeal. From the perspective of an American media consumer, the image of Mandela is the image of a black man and thus hardly distinguishable from any senior African American – he becomes "one of us" or "one of them" depending on where one is located ideologically. Viewers with a deeper knowledge recognized him as the member of the ANC, incarcerated for twenty-seven years because of his opposition to apartheid.

After his release, however, the man who was no longer silent, who answered questions in his way irrespective of what prior perceptions interviewers and audiences may hold, became far more concrete. Mandela shifted in people's imagination from a veiled presence exerting silent influence, towards becoming a person with particular associations, who is connected in real terms with actual events. In short, the media attention unleashed by Mandela's release broke a long continuity of perception about South Africa. Where Fox, certainly driven by marketing needs in its bid to secure African-American viewership, could find the means to provide six hours of coverage of the *FreedomFest* concert, the events of 1990 shifted attention because they had demonstrated that the assumed continuity of interest between American and black South Africans was very tenuous indeed. Mandela and the ANC were not quite the HBO authentic African chieftain-ministers hierarchy everyone perhaps thought they would turn out to be. The actual negotiations process revealed that what Mandela and the ANC stood for was far more aligned with other issues than merely another black-white confrontation.

Continuity and Change: On Becoming a Genuine Icon

Prior to his release, Mandela can be seen to have embodied certain qualities that are valued across cultural boundaries. His very silence and photographic absence during twenty-seven years of imprisonment, meshed with ongoing awareness of his survival as reported through various channels (above and below ground), itself presented something of the qualities of endurance, perseverance, and steadfastness. The same silence, as a physical removal of his voice from the ears of the world, ensured that as a sign it would be impossible to pin any specific meaning onto the very qualities that silence showed. Indeed, the imprisoned Mandela was iconic in the most literal sense even if his photographic likeness was absent, banned from the media for a generation. He signified qualities prior to any definite demonstration of them, or any actual accomplishment based on them.

In semiotic terms, Mandela as a sign was iconic in the sense that he was just what he was. On the other hand, his image could determine any number of symbols to the extent that others in different contexts could connect this image indexically with something. If being human ("Man") is itself a sign, as Peirce argued, then clearly the predominantly iconic sign that used to be "being-Mandela" has become far more significant than the aircraft silhouette that announces "being-airport," but can never specify *which* airport. After the breaking of the silence, however, the very cultural plurality of the modern world reasserted itself. Different societies and different communities responded to Mandela not as a pure, self-sufficient icon but as a sign that responded to iconic qualities proper to their *own* contexts and political and racial struggles.

As a person in a particular cultural-political environment, making significant statements and performing tasks proper to the habits of that environment, Mandela quickly became more significant in indexical and symbolic terms. Put differently, he made his own statements and could (and did) correct those who misrepresented them, as opposed to previously, when mention of "Mandela" permitted all who heard it to make any determination of it they chose to make. A speaking and answering Mandela, in other words, is a sign that has a far more limited range of symbolic determination than the silent presence that was in itself wholly undetermined.

The presence or image of Mandela had once been capable of being pitched to any key, or adopted by consensus (settled by vote, so to speak) for the many people in diverse communities that make up the media audience. By the time of the *Tribute* concert the same image and presence had begun to develop limits to its interpretability. This had come about precisely because the icon had once again come to speak, to pitch itself to a key, to participate in and influence the vote. In effect, the icon had finally regained its connection with the index and the symbol.

For a Mandela to serve as a cultural icon in the sense outlined above, he (or she) should not have too distinct a voice. Thus the iconic status of Winnie Mandela also evolved out of her enforced silence as a banned person; it would not be too much to say that she retains more iconicity than her former husband because of her very distinct political marginalization after 1994. Icons indicate qualities and their continuity; symbols are determined, "fixed to be *this* (or *thus*), in contradistinction to being this, that, or the other (or in some way or other)" (Peirce vol. 6, 1965–66: 625). Once personal iconic personalities (re)gain a voice, as happened to Mandela in 1990, other people lose control over assigning meaning.

In contrast with the experience of the *Tribute* concert organizers' experience with the broadcast media, when Mandela had indeed regained his capacity to determine what he said, the following, said about the *FreedomFest*, is illuminating:

> Anti-Apartheid could not lose. The cause did not obscure the culture, they embraced one-another. The essence of Mandela and his imprisonment, through the celebration of his birthday, had itself become an entertainment event. Cause and celebration were indistinguishable. The opponents, meanwhile, distinguished themselves as antiquated killjoys lost in the mists of parliamentary politicking, while everyone else was simply intent on having a party. (Perryman 1988: 31)

Before his release, Mandela's presence and image ("idea") effectively could be seen to have affected two broad aggregations: those with the Anti-Apartheid Movement, and those not with the movement. *FreeedomFest* quite perfectly realized the multiplicity of determinations that a genuine iconic sign can generate. Some of the participating groups themselves – Salt 'n Pepa, for example – even admitted ignorance as to who Mandela was (Fisher 1989: 41). All that counted was the party.

After 1990, media took a different figure, one with a voice, to the same audience, but the voice had smashed the homogeneity of community that the silent figure had conferred earlier. The icon now acted, had ways of doing and saying that the many aggregations that make up "the audience" could hear for themselves. What they could also see for themselves was a fully developed, and still-developing, sign in its own right. Since South Africa's democracy was accomplished in 1994, this new and autonomous sign has, along with the new South African flag, come to represent the idea of racial reconciliation and unity: the New South Africa as Africa's success story. The *46664* concert held in South Africa in November 2003 is as good a contrast with the iconic Mandela of before 1990 as one can find. More than another highly publicized media event organized around the figure of Nelson Mandela, the concert and surrounding campaign demonstrate Mandela's deliberate use of his previously iconic status to gain international support for a new cause. In the process he has become even more powerfully symbolic in his power to fix the iconicism of other signs, in this case, HIV/AIDS.

The concert was the flagship event of the *46664 "Give one minute of your life to AIDS"* campaign, initiated by the Nelson Mandela Foundation to create awareness of HIV/AIDS through the most widely distributed and broadcast musical program on AIDS to date. In addition to the concert and its attendant CD and DVD, the campaign included a global telephone petition and a music launch on the web. The five-hour concert featured international musicians such as Beyoncé, The Corrs, David Bowie, and Eurythmics and drew a crowd of 40,000 people to the Cape Town stadium where it was held. Global internet service providers and music portals worked with host company Tiscali to provide the biggest free global web broadcast in history (BBC 2003/11/29). A reported 1,200,000 computer users logged on to view the concert. Highlights of the event were distributed copyright-free, and broadcast by the South African Broadcasting Corporation, the European Broadcasting Union, the Asian Broadcasting Union, and MTV. BBC World Service Radio also broadcast the concert in thirteen languages across thirty-seven countries. In all, the concert was expected to reach a global audience of more than 2 billion people in 166 countries.

The campaign and concert reveal how Mandela's current role of statesman enables him to exploit the public iconicity of his personal narrative of incarceration under apartheid, to act as an independent symbol to gain support for the HIV/AIDS cause. For example, the campaign strapline "46664" originates in Mandela's prison identity number. Indeed, Mandela mobilized his now well-developed symbolic powers to persuade campaign organizers to use this number globally for the petition phone numbers, and to include it in the campaign theme song titled "Long Walk to Freedom" (Stewart and Strummer 2004). Similarly, campaign advertisements featured Mandela's face alongside the 46664 prison/campaign number, in a highly symbolic assertion of his public status. The concert also featured a large statue of Mandela's head on the performance stage, highlighting once again the now-symbolic quality of the face that, in its previously conjectured features, had been the vague and undetermined icon of nearly every international movement that sought somebody's freedom. In this way, Mandela's face has become to the international audience the marker of almost any symbolic assertion about rights and freedom.

Indeed, the *46664* concert demonstrates well the way in which symbols grow. Where Mandela's pre-release symbolism had tended to lie in the statements of others, in the sense that his absent image worked as a kind of logical universal quantifier of freedom and liberation, the concert became in itself Mandela's statement of commitment to causes that involve the plight of others. Where the antiapartheid movements used Mandela iconically to frame their arguments against whatever local agendas activists may have perceived as supporting apartheid, Mandela quite consciously used his symbolic influence to mobilize musicians and activists to action on the iconic quantifiers that are constituted by the reality of HIV and AIDS. The association of this suffering with South Africa, ironically enough, permitted Mandela to lend his symbolic value to what media commentator Jeremy Maggs (2003: 6) views as "the burgeoning Brand SA [South Africa]." Thus Maggs's point that Mandela has "crossed the perception threshold from a personality to a brand" in public awareness reinforces his highly symbolic value as an argument for (or representation of) the virtues associated with overcoming suffering in general.

Mandela's new symbolism, his now-independent signifying capacity, further played out in his corralling of powerful people to support the concert. Among these were global business players (BBC, Virgin, Coca Cola), international figures (Bill Clinton, Tony Blair, Oprah Winfrey) and entertainment celebrities. Mandela's standing among them therefore contributed to the scale of the show, ensuring that other cultural and pop culture icons would transmit South Africa's plight to a global audience, creating a global "imagined community" of supporters.

Conclusion

Growth is a different kind of continuity to the constancy entailed in iconicity. When a group or class or aggregation of people claims continuity in some iconic sense, there needs to be a continuous presence of three generations to whom can be ascribed at least those iconic qualities that fall under the accomplishment to date of "culture." However, the continuity of culture is contingent on the presence of people who can demonstrate their belonging to an aggregation in the present, and usually into a more or less indefinite past as well. Mandela is clearly such a person in the perception of a global community, as the success of the *46664* concert shows.

It should therefore be reasonably clear that continuity itself is a quality that applies in special ways to the conceptions of icons and of cultures, but that in a pragmaticist analysis share the same kind of continuity. Where icons serve specifically to indicate the quality of continuity in the functional relations between sign and object in a broad sense of logic, culture is indicative of a quality of continuity arising specifically in the context of the reproduction of contingent human aggregations. Mandela can still have iconic status, but this can only (for the present, anyway) occur within specific and even rather limited aggregations. On the other hand, his massively symbolic presence since 1994 demonstrates the very essence of how iconic constancy can remain at the root of symbolic growth. Mandela's fortitude, perseverance, and steadfastness in a specific political context will continue to inspire people who are part of comparable contexts to point to these qualities as examples. His future impact as a symbol, in the sense embodied in the organization of the 2003 concert, is yet to be determined.

Notes

1. We base the discussion of this example on Sudderth (1990).
2. This example is based on Tomaselli and Boster (1993).
3. This example is taken from Tomaselli and Tomaselli (1990).

References

Brown, T. (1980). "Did Anyone Know his Name?" Coverage of Steve Biko and the Black Consciousness Movement in South Africa by the *New York Times* and the *Washington Post*, 1969–1977. *Ecquid Novi* 1(1): 29–49.

Dineslow, R. (1989). The Biggest Political Pop Show in History. In *When the Music's Over: The Story of Political Pop*. London: Faber and Faber.

Fisher, K. (1989). *Singing a Song for Freedom: An Examination of the 'Free Nelson Mandela' 70th Birthday Concert at Wembley*. Unpublished Undergraduate Dissertation. Center for Cultural Studies, University of Birmingham.

Gabriel, P. (1980). "Biko". *Melt*. Geffen Records.

Maggs, J. (2003). Measuring Brand Mandela. *Upfront: Southern African Executive Life*, August, 6.

Moodie, T. D. (1975). *The Rise of Afrikanerdom: Power, Apartheid, and the Afrikaner Civil Religion*. Berkeley: University of California Press.

Peirce, C. S. (1965–66). *The Collected Papers of Charles Sanders Peirce. Vols. I–VI*, C. Harteshorne and P. Weiss. (eds.). Vol. 6, A. W. Burks. (ed.). Cambridge, MA: Harvard University Press.

Perryman, M. (1988). The Mandela Moment. *Marxism Today*, September, 28–31.

Ransdell, J. M. (1997). On Peirce's Conception of the Iconic Sign. Modified version of article originally published in P. Bouissac, M. Herzfeld, and R. Posner (eds.), *Iconicity: Essays on the Nature of Culture, Festschrift for Thomas A. Sebeok*. Berlin: Stauffenburg Verlag.

Sampson, J. (2003). "Brand Mandela – Priceless". *Upfront: South African Executive Life*. August 2003: 22.

Shepperson, A. (1995). *On the Social Interpretation of Cultural Experience: Reflections on Raymond Williams's Early Cultural Writings (1958–1963)*. Durban: University of Natal. http://www.und.ac.za/und/ccms/articles/culture.htm.

The Special AKA. (1984). "Free Nelson Mandela." *In the Studio*. 2-Tone Records.

Stewart, D. A, and Strummer, J. (2004). "Long Walk to Freedom." *46664*. Warner Records.

Sudderth, W. (1990). Critique of *Mandela*. Directed by Philip Saville. (1987). Home Box Office. 120 minutes. Retrieved from: http://ccms.ukzn.ac.za.

Tomaselli, K. G. and Boster, B. (1993). Mandela, MTV, Television and Apartheid. *Popular Music and Society* 17(2): 1–19.

Tomaselli, K. G. and Tomaselli, R. E. (1990). The Media and Mandela. *Transafrica Forum* 7(2): 55–66.

Tomaselli, K. G. and Teer-Tomaselli, R. E. (2003). The Media and Mandela. *Safundi* 4(2): 1–10.

Williams, R. (1958). *Culture and Society, 1780–1950.* London and New York: Columbia University Press.

———. (1965). *Culture and Society.* Harmondsworth, UK: Pelican.

Websites

http://www.46664.tiscali.com

http://www.bbc.co.uk

Video/Filmography

Attenborough, R. (Director) (1987). *Cry Freedom* [film]. Marble Arch Productions.

Feinberg, B. (Director) (1988). *Free Mandela* [Video]. IDAF.

Nelson Mandela Tribute. (1990). [Video]. Tribute Productions.

Saville, P. (Director) (1987). *Mandela.* [TV series]. HBO.

THE LITTLE MERMAID

Finn Hauberg Mortensen

Beginnings and Ending

Simple symbols seldom carry singular meanings. For example, in ancient Rome, "Ianua" meant a door, pure and simple. Yet the door to the Forum Romanum was a symbol: it was closed during times of peace and was left open while the Roman soldiers were at war. The door served as a concrete expression of the boundary between the safety of home and the turbulent world outside. From its position in the gatehouse of the Forum wall, the door was watched over by its divine guardian Janus. Placed thus, Janus's two faces were able to gaze towards the east and the west; the beginning and the end of the unknown. The Romans named the first month after him, and he was worshipped the first day of every month as well as in the early morning. Just as birth was his department, so too were new inventions and acts, among them communication. Naturally, the god of beginnings had no parents, but he certainly had predecessors. Before Janus came Hermes.

Hermes was the protector of wayfarers and the defender of entrances. In early Greek culture, cairns and pillars indicated boundaries and roads. These were later replaced with *herms*, four-sided stone posts depicting one or more faces, which were meant to subdue the foreign through magic. Gradually these herms were adorned with the suggestion of arms and a phallus, and later the entire torso was reworked artistically. The result was the individualized portrait bust, used at gymnasiums as a model for young practitioners of the grace of the body. So, with the introduction of the herm, stone heaps and pillars were replaced with an idol representing a human being.

However, Hermes was not the beginning of the beginning in Western culture. The Egyptians regarded Thot as Hermes' predecessor and the mission of both gods was to transport humans to the kingdom of the dead and to settle their accounts. Frequently, Thot is seen in hieroglyphs as the holy and immortal Ibis, who in his life waged a continual battle against evil. This animism in the early stages of civilization is again found in cave paintings and is understood as an expression of the magical power of animals and prey.

The hunt for beginnings thus appears to end with people's need to control their own fears by establishing a boundary between the known and the unknown. "The beginning" is a search for beginning: it is both empty and value determined. This is also suggested in the etymological definition of the word *world* and can be traced back to the Germanic compound of the words for *man* and *age* ("verr" and "old" in Old Norse); that is, "man's age" or "man's memory." The designation, then, had to do with time and not space: the time an individual has to learn through memory and experience and to enter into the foreign (meaning a stage of development, a cultural tradition, class, or gender).

The individual's effort to understand "the beginning" corresponds to the formation of a cosmology by the cultural collective, a process that consists of inserting meaning into *chaos*, the Greek word for gap or chasm. Every culture rests upon a cosmology and, despite cross-cultural differences, these cosmologies appear to share a number of striking traits. First and foremost, the end is made into the beginning by deducing the unknown from known results in a reverse construction that is grounded in the need for an understanding of the whole. Stories of genesis are about grasping the beginning of a story that is capable of providing legitimacy and instructions for action in the individual's historical process – a protective refuge of a superindividual nature. It is no coincidence that Thot, Hermes, and Janus had in common the power over language.

Hesiod's *Theogony*, the earliest Greek cosmology, relates that at the beginning of the world, chaos existed as a static and disorderly space from which the earth, stars, sky, and ocean arose. In the Old Testament, God establishes with his words of creation the division between light and darkness, sky and water, land and ocean, animals and plants, woman and man. These divisions enabled the transformation from an all-encompassing and preexistent chaos into its opposite – a dynamic, cosmic order. Everything would then be in order – or so it would seem. The catch, however, is that cultural history has been filled with Janus-like creatures with bifurcated bodies that are at once god and human; human and animal. One such figure is the little mermaid in Hans Christian Andersen's fairy tale of the same name.

With roots in the animistic remains of their earlier traditions, the Greeks made the gods into relatives of more or less perfect human beings whose controversies (as depicted by Homer) could intervene in the skewed course of things down below. Repeatedly, philosophers attempted to undermine such anthropomorphism. Xenophon claimed, for example, that if horses and oxen were given the opportunity to picture their gods, these gods would most likely resemble horses and oxen. Although the first Christian thinkers made a clear distinction, along similar lines, between human beings and a single God who had replaced a host of human-like gods, the heirs of these relatives would make a powerful comeback. Indeed, in its practical attempts to spread God's word, the Church made use of a comprehensive gallery of human deities.

Characterizing religion as the intermediary between mortal sinners and an immortal and infallible God, the anthropologist Edmund Leach wrote that in myths, the most important cult objects are embodied deities or deified humans, such as Jesus and the Virgin Mary, rather than the unapproachable prima causa (Fausing and Larsen 1980, author translation). In 1600, Giordano Bruno was burned as a heretic after his attack on ecclesiastical anthropomorphism. He envisaged an infinite universe without center, with God situated beyond all human recognition. In the middle of the next century, Spinoza was also branded a heretic because he applied pantheistic ideas in his arguments claiming that the concept of God was irreconcilable with all human laws and activities. The danger in Renaissance humanism's attack on anthropomorphism lay in its separation of nature and culture from the divine. The ultimate consequence of this was twofold. On the one hand, human beings in Western culture might now be regarded as free and innovative creatures; on the other hand, science duplicated religion's role as a marker between the known and the unknown. Religion's boundary between this world and the hereafter could now be understood as a difference between faith and knowledge. Within the field of science, a decisive line could then be drawn between the known and the as-yet unknown, which, in principle, could be conquered and would be conquered in the future. From this research front, researchers have since been called into battle against the unknown.

Despite bouts of reformatory iconoclasm, the Church continued to illustrate the unknown through embodied deities and deified humans. Philosophers' critiques of this projection continued up to and including Hegel's left-wing critique of religion, which emphasized that human needs were not a tool for understanding the beyond, but rather the very basis for *the beyond* in its radical sense. With the move from anthropomorphism to modern science, humankind was left with an invisible or dead god, a positivism that claimed the ability to reveal all things in due course. In short, humankind was left with itself as its greatest conundrum.

The dualism between humankind and God is portrayed in one of the most prominent works commissioned by the Catholic Church, Michelangelo's *Creation*, painted on the ceiling of the Sistine Chapel in approximately 1510. The three initial frescoes portray God in his cosmos without humans, the last three scenes show humankind's depraved world without God, while the three middle scenes depict an imaginary paradise in which humans talk to both God and the Devil. In the very middle, we see Eve, who is also the Virgin Mary – the second Eve – just as Adam is also Christ, the second Adam. In its entirety, the suite reconstructs perdition as a necessary conclusion to creation. The suggestion of chaos that is conveyed can then be received by the spectator as an upwardly directed prayer for absolution. According to Leach, Michelangelo conceived of God as a Janus figure: "God is the borderland; he is that whole which is both itself and its non-self"(as cited in Fausing and Larsen 1980). This complex entity may be understood as an absolute beginning, but it contains a memory of disorderly static chaos in the darkness and a dynamic pointing ahead in the light. The beginning thereby appears as a process in time between opposites that are mutually dependent upon each other. It is dynamic, but the division is fixed.

The dualism between God and humans is often perceived as dualism between the divine and the animal within us. Since ancient times, supernatural creatures have been a standard element in widely different cultures. Western culture has depicted a series of combinations of animal bodies whose qualities have been recombined by the human imagination into a force beyond nature. A griffin is thus a winged animal with the head of a raptor and the body of a carnivore. Among this colorful number of bifurcated creatures – the basilisk, chimera, dragon, unicorn, merman, hydra, centaur, cyclops, medusa, roc, satyr, sphinx, vampire, and werewolf – there are some that are different from the rest in that they combine a human body with an animal one. For example, the sphinx is often attributed with wings, a human head, and a lion's body. The Egyptian and West Asian traditions associated with this awe-inspiring monster subsequently merged with the local legends of ancient Greece, which explains why the sphinx occupies a considerable role in the Theban cycle of legends and in the Oedipus tragedies.

In Greek folklore, sirens belong to this category of supernatural creatures. With their womanly face and bird's body, they lured sailors towards the shore and caused them to run aground. Homer's *Odyssey* recounts how the hero Odysseus allows himself to be bound to the mast during his homeward journey in order to avoid being seduced by the sirens. Presumably, the original source behind the Greek belief in mermaids is in fact the sea cow, a member of the mammalian order related to the elephant and known as "Sirenia." During the nursing period, these animals develop full breasts in their armpits, and, with their rudimentary hind limbs, they can appear as a naturally occurring bifurcated body with the upper body of a hoofed animal and the lower body of a fish or a whale. Since they come very close to the shore to feed on eelgrass and other plants and can grow more than three meters long, it is very likely that these sirens were the real object of sailors' attentions and terror.[1]

If our need to create meaning leads to the construction of divine creatures that are at once human and superhuman, then it would seem plausible to imagine that we also have a need to explore human nature, particularly our own drives, and we do so when we see such drives reflected in the qualities found in animals or attributed to them. The animal in humans is understood as the human in animals, not least in modern society in which projections of specific human characteristics have been rerouted from paganism's divine relatives and Catholicism's saints to those animals that we most associate with ourselves and worship like modern idols. Although mermaids are not the holy creatures that cows are in India or dogs are in the West, despite the fact that they may have been based on the sea cow, these creatures were the imaginative constructions arising from specific encounters, constructions whose beginnings can be found in the human need to understand sexuality and love.

Folk Culture and Mass Culture

On its way to the sea, the Odense River runs sluggishly through the city. The riverbed is not very deep. Here, in the cold water, Andersen's mother stood and washed clothes for the wealthy. In 1855 he depicted this scene in "She was Good for Nothing," (Andersen 1930) which tells of a kind-hearted mother who dies from the cold and toil. Twenty years earlier, he had placed the setting of another of his fairy tales, "Little Claus and Big Claus" (Andersen 1930) by the same river. In the story, Little Claus, the sharp and cunning proletarian, settles accounts with the superior powers that be and finally fools Big Claus into letting himself be drowned, tempted as he is by the fine sea cattle that are to be found at the bottom of the river. In later Nordic folklore, sea cattle belonged to the merpeople and were thereby associated with mermen and sea giants who were believed to be the cause of accidents at sea. Nordic folklore also contained bifurcated bodies that were half-woman and half-fish. They were first mentioned in medieval folk ballads and later became part of the fabric of the legends of feudal traditional culture in which they were most often depicted as the friendly helpers of sailors.

Andersen's tale "The Little Mermaid" was written in 1836–37 and first published on 7 April 1837. Although the author maintained that his work had no model, the tale nonetheless draws on the traditions of an older feudal oral folk culture. Earlier, folk ballads had supplied Danish authors such as Johannes Ewald with mermaid material, and Andersen himself had already used such material in a number of works. Among these was "Agnete and the Merman," from 1833, in which the merman figure asserts that Agnete can only receive an immortal soul through her love. "The Little Mermaid" is also inspired by contemporary works. Part of the plot is borrowed from the Danish author B. S. Ingemann's *The Creatures from the Underworld* (1817), while the mermaid's longing for an immortal soul and the ultimate transformation of her body into sea foam derives from a fairy tale entitled *Undine* (1811), by the German author Friedrich de la Motte Fouqué. Clearly, then, Andersen's text contributes to the comprehensive reconstitution and intermedial transformation of traditional culture that occurred during the Romantic period.

A complicated field of meanings unfolds in connection with the mermaid. For instance, Andersen draws on several kinds of sources. In addition, there are many other works on mermaids from Andersen's time that may also serve as a basis for the reconstitution and intermedial transformation of this figure by mass culture in more recent times. Such problems are beyond the scope of the present chapter, the premise of which is that this fairy tale text in particular had qualities that caused the course of tradition to change, and that it was this text specifically that served as material for modern industrial mass culture. A more detailed discussion of these propositions will not be possible here, however, since I wish to concentrate instead on an analysis of the text and its intermedial transformation in Walt Disney's hands. Disney draws indisputably on Andersen's fairy tale. Although the field of meanings and understandings presupposes the original tale, it appears only in the form of reconstructions and repetitions – intermedial transformations that both give meaning and take meaning away.

The Disney film relates not only to the text, but also to the sculpture purchased in 1913 by the founder of the Carlsberg brewery, Carl Jacobsen, and erected at Langelinje in Copenhagen. The artist, Edvard Eriksen, rather innocently depicted dancer Ellen Price with a mermaid's tail and placed the figure on a flat stone near the pier. He was also inspired by Frenchman Henri Chapu's *Jeanne d'Arc* sculpture from 1870, a replica of which had been erected in Copenhagen. However, Eriksen's mermaid is not simply a sculpture. Although a diminutive height of 1.25 meters, it is a national monument that is undoubtedly associated with Andersen. At the same time, it has become detached from its author and stands today both as a symbol for Denmark in general and Copenhagen in particular. It has also acted as the springboard for intermedial transformations that are only remotely connected to Andersen, although they play a significant role in today's folk culture; that is, the tourist and culture industry. While

Eriksen's mermaid longs wistfully (or tragically) for a love that cannot be realized, a steady stream of postcards and merchandise generally manage to portray her as little more than a reference to the fact that Denmark was the first country to lift the criminal ban on pornographic pictures (1969) or as representative of the stereotypical blonde Scandinavian beauty.

One frequently sees examples of how the mermaid is ascribed with a sexual meaning – far removed from the works of both Andersen and Eriksen – in advertisements, pictures, and articles in the media. One such example is the large-scale billboard advertisements found throughout Rome a few years ago that depicted a bifurcated mermaid body whose female nether regions were merged with half a banana, the peel of which was slit slightly upwards at the bottom. Evidently, this practical combination of one male and one female sexual attribute was meant to sell more banana yoghurt. Two stories published in Danish newspapers on the day that this article was written also come to mind (*Fyens Stiftstidende* and *Politiken*, 17 August 2003). First, a report on the gay pride parade, "Danish Mermaid Pride," which was criticized by a lesbian group who argued that homosexuality should not be displayed as something unique or unusual. Second, a story about Weeki Wachee, Florida, a water park that has fallen on hard times despite the fact that generations of young girls once fought to be allowed to appear there, dressed in a mermaid costume and submerged in a gigantic glass tank before half a million visitors each year.

In 1964, however, another more sophisticated meaning was attributed to the monument. Paradoxically, its status was underscored after the statue was defaced by a steady array of unknown perpetrators who sawed off the mermaid's head and carried it away. Pictures of the defaced statue were seen the world over, and the event marked the beginning of a new wave of intermedial transformation. These pranks were arranged by an until then relatively unknown situationist, Jørgen Nash, who kept the migrating tale in motion when he declared himself guilty of "mermaid murder" in 1998. While the amount of media attention this case received was central to the way in which events unfolded, it is debatable whether or not Nash is correct when he claims that these events rekindled interest in Andersen's fairy tale. A quick glance at the many tourist shots taken daily of the mermaid on Langelinje, the professional tourist merchandise available, and the "mermaid murder" happening suggests, rather, that these phenomena represent different forms of dilution – the breakdown of tradition – from the perspective of Andersen's text and are an expression of the fact that the mermaid is now living in a modern, industrialized folk culture.

From a historical consciousness perspective, the long chain of references that have established the mermaid as a structure of meaning over time can be divided into three layers: the feudal-popular-pagan traditional culture with its superstitious sailors and folk ballads with sea creatures; the bourgeois-Christian culture to which both Andersen's fairy tale and Eriksen's statue at Copenhagen's harbor belong; and finally, mass culture with its multimedia exploitation of Andersen's fairy tale, the most characteristic example of which is Disney's (Clements and Musker 1989) postmodern animated musical. The issue, then, is what each of the three layers refers to and which *tertium comparationis* – common point of resemblance – makes each individual reference possible, as well as whether these three different layers refer to each other to form an interwoven, multiple structure of meaning – and, if so, how. Given the scope of the present chapter, it is not possible to examine these problems now – problems that have been essential in the humanities since the first transfer of traditions at the library in Alexandria, and throughout the Renaissance, in part because we cannot escape the fact that we must also use ourselves as a standard when we assume possession of other cultural traditions. This involves transformation. In what follows, I will focus on one such transfer in an attempt to analyze Andersen's fairy tale and its intermedial transformation in Disney's film.

Hans Christian Andersen's Mermaid

Space and Setting

The "space" of this fairy tale is highly economic in its construction. Vertically, it is organized through an opposition between up and down, sky and seabed. Between these two, there lies a third level that is organized horizontally through an opposition between sea surface and dry land. The story takes place on this horizontal plane, and while it is standard mermaid custom to lure sailors downwards from this land to sea, the little mermaid, in contrast, strives with her good deeds to achieve immortality and move heavenwards (Clements and Musker 1989). In short, the space is composed of four positions: up, down, land, water.

The text is a frame story, that is, a story about a story. This is clear in the introduction, in which the listeners are transported from the moment of storytelling in the sitting room, far out to sea where the actual events take place, and, from there, down to the bottom of the sea. The dualism between frame and central story is also thematized at those points in the text where the narrator describes plants and creatures from the deep as phenomena from contemporary daily life. In so doing, a model from contemporary life is also imposed on the merpeople. These moves are discrete, and are well known from other fairy tales by Andersen, but this story differs from the others since here the scene is placed in the frame, and the two stories then overlap. In the final paragraph the actors become "the Daughters of the Air" whom the little mermaid has joined and whose good deeds and hopes for an eternal life are projections from the ground level. What is up and what is down are determined from this point onwards.

The daughters of the air keep watch from above and turn the children listening to the story into actors in the emancipation process that the daughters must undergo. When the children behave well towards their parents, the trial period of the daughters is shortened, whereas naughtiness will lengthen the trial period. This kind of activation of the audience is analogous to a modern computer game in which the recipient is able to choose his or her own way through the plot. This resemblance is only superficial, however, since the choice is between ethical and unethical acts in the bosom of one's family rather than cost-free choices in a fictional universe.

Many regard the finale as a moral seemingly tacked on after the fact. However, both the gradual revelation of the tale's frame and the very genesis of the tale could lead one to dispute this view. While still in the process of writing, the author referred to the text as "The Daughters of the Sea." Prior to this, in a letter to Andersen, a friend referred to the text as "The Daughters of the Air," which would suggest that this part of the story served as a point of departure (Dal 1990, 7: 37). Another argument in favor of interpreting the final paragraph as an organic part of the text is that the surprise ending of the main story – the mermaid's ascent to the ethereal sphere and with it the possibility of obtaining an immortal soul – is overshadowed by the fact that the children listening to the narrative are the true actors in this Christian-moral field of meaning. What child would not want to be on their best behavior if this would put an end to the heroine's sufferings in the bedtime story papa just read and laid on the bedside table?

With its focus on children's behavior, this interactive fairy tale is similar to the surveillance texts typical of children's literature before the leap forward that Andersen was a part of (Simonsen 1942: 42ff; on surveillance literature see Ariès 1982). The novelty of this focus lies, as it does in the mermaid story, in the tale's regulation of behavior through internal control. Rebellious children are not punished corporally by a distant, severe father (deity), but learn instead to feel sorrow and shame as well as a sense of responsibility for ensuring that innocent representatives of goodness are not punished.

Many have argued that the prince is in fact the main character of the tale (Barlby 1994: 69ff). Certainly, he is at the center of the story of human longing for incorporation into the strange, fertile sea element that is embedded within the tale about this mermaid–girl-child. The longing that *she* feels is more justified, however, because it results in character development the very moment the knife strikes the surface of the water. The prince is left longing, but self-reflexive. He is neither action nor character and is therefore unable to accomplish the task assigned to the children in the frame story: to give others an "eternal soul" through love. This is conveyed most concretely in terms of the children's responsibility to love and obey their parents. Parents in turn are actively involved in reading the tale aloud to their children.

The child's solicitous love for its parents replaces the mermaid's awakening consciousness of her sexual drives as the key to the divine. The main story tells of a broken nuclear family at the bottom of the sea where the children are attributed with a divine power for controlling the demons of the sea. However, instead of transporting its listeners to the realm of superstition, this fairy tale transforms them into actors in the fiction and reinterprets demonic nature, thus returning them back to their real lives to choose between good and evil, happiness and tragedy.

Soul and Gender

The story of the little mermaid follows the structure of a Bildungsroman, both in terms of its framing and narration: from (1) childhood in the family, via (2) the quandaries of youth: the discovery of humans – "the other nature" – to (3) a mature actualization of self among "the Daughters of the Air." It begins and ends happily, but, as usual, the story focuses on an intervening schism. In this case, the shifts between sky and sea that are duplicated in the relationship between dry land and sea floor, as well as the ruptures between good and evil, produce the sort of mistaken identity moments and gory scenes that are found in late-Romantic opera.

After reading the story soon after its publication, Danish author Carsten Hauch wondered at the little creature's ability to follow her own instincts toward the good so purposefully without already possessing the eternal soul she so yearned for.[2] Had she lacked this drive, however, the story would have been about evil. Instead, it deals with the relationship between the temporal and the eternal in a process of development necessary for taking possession of oneself. The children's literature that dominated the period up until pre-Romanticism did not attribute to the child an innate divine soul. Instead, the child would acquire one and become human once its wild nature had been disciplined. Both Kierkegaard and Andersen moved beyond this point. Although the mermaid is not human, both she and children in general are assumed to possess the instinct to do good from the outset. Indeed, an upbringing based on internal control would not be possible otherwise.

The mermaid comes from a family sphere devoid of sexuality. Her father is a widower. His mother, who fills in for the absent mother in the good mother role, knows more about the life of humans than she reveals to her grandchildren when, in their encounter with the unfamiliar, they also encounter their own sexual identity. She brings the girls face-to-face with the opposition between sea surface and dry land – the site of the drama – so that they, like her, will choose to be encapsulated in their own seamless nature. They receive a comfortable and merry life of three hundred years, but no immortal soul. The youngest of the girls is an exception. From the very start, her longing makes her different, and she attempts to receive an eternal soul through the realization of her love for a human being. A Faust in reverse, she must sell half of her body as well as her voice to the sea witch, whose appearance, stronghold, and underwater servants identify her as the figure to which the sum of underwater sexuality has been driven – masculine sexuality, in particular (if we are to believe the phallic nature symbols). The description of the sea witch ought to please every Freudian, who can then ponder the degree to which she represents the masculine in the story: the demonic helper who exceeds the demonic – a feat neither the sea king nor the land prince is capable of.

The process is irreversible and the terms harsh: in order to obtain an eternal soul, the prince must be so in love with her that he forgets the existence of both his father and his mother and marries the little mermaid (Clements and Musker 1989). This is not only the higher goal, but also the overarching one. As everyone knows, the project fails. Despite his intuitive love for the one that saved him, the prince sees her as his "little foundling" and does not understand the language left to her.

She strives for both the red and the white; the use of color symbols is but one of the effective devices in the text (e.g., the sun, flowers, etc. versus the swans, snow, marble, foam). After the little mermaid's sisters, in a sacrificial gesture, offer the sea witch their glorious hair in exchange for a knife with which their little sister can re-enter the fold, the little mermaid turns the water blood-red. She does this not by plunging it into the heart of the newlywed prince, but by turning the weapon on herself. Liberation lies in this self-sacrifice. She has taken life like a man (the phallic knife) in an instinctive act in which the body is (again) offered on behalf of the spirit. Like Aphrodite in reverse, her body dissolves into white foam, and she is united with those "transparent, beautiful beings" floating in the air, who are invisible to humans: "their voice was melodious, but so ethereal that no human ear was able to hear it" (Dal 1990).

As is often the case in Andersen's tales, the little mermaid – as a figure of righteousness – receives yet another chance: the set of sisters who had a sea life consisting of three hundred years of familiar comfort are replaced with another set of sisters for whom a trial period of three hundred years awaits. This is an example of deferred gratification with a vengeance, or a case of the Protestant work ethic as outlined by Max Weber. The children of the air and those of the living room are only able to communicate through good deeds, so one presumes that the trial period is not yet over. Andersen's text is, then, a *Bildungstale* about the mermaid enclosed within a conduct story addressed to children of the time. It continues to tell us something about the discovery of the child via internal control, and reimprinting by way of the subconscious.

The demons are put into words and can then be countered with actions that simultaneously reduce religion to ethics just as sexuality is removed from love. Subsequently, virtue and love for one's parents are able to stand guard together over home life as abstract representatives for actual parental surveillance of children. In the process, Andersen certainly shows bravery and daring in his fascinating account of sexual longing that finds expression during the child's meeting with itself as an adult. Readers have seen enough within and between the lines to grasp both how much is implied in them and why – by land, by sea, and by air.

Disney's Mermaid

Children's culture has long been part of mass culture, both when it was religious and later under the aegis of market forces. It is therefore not surprising that Disney, the most powerful international brand for children's culture, adapted "The Little Mermaid" for a global audience. It is a question, then, of an act of intermedial transformation with explicit reference to Andersen's text. The latter is just as ill protected against reinterpretation and distortion as the folk literary tradition was when Andersen seized hold of it. Although I certainly find it relevant to evaluate the film on its own artistic and commercial premises, I will have to limit myself in what follows to an examination of the film's reconstitution of Andersen's fairy tale.

Disney's film was released in Denmark in the fall of 1990, to much anticipation, after a launch using every means available to the modern media industry. It was to be Disney's great comeback to the animated musical film. The firm had already supplied a number of brilliant examples of this genre as early as the 1930s, and with *Snow White* in 1937, Disney enjoyed unprecedented artistic and economic success. Andersen's work had already been the subject of an earlier Disney film, *The Ugly Duckling* (1939), and after a series of lean years, the American version of *The Little Mermaid* more than fulfilled artistic expectations, receiving Oscars for best music and best song. The Danish version of the film was dubbed using the voices and singing talents of eminent domestic artists.

A large-scale public relations campaign was set in motion before the film appeared on the screen. Children were encouraged to persuade their parents to purchase posters, records, erasers, pencils, action figures, and burgers at McDonald's – all in the name of the mermaid. And after that, these same adults could invest a tidy sum of money in collector's pictures taken from the film (placed in an album that was itself extremely inexpensive) in an attempt to trick as many people as possible into taking the imaginative leap. Together with these additional products, the film was sold as the central component in a concept demanding the total attention of consumers, along the lines of the *Teenage Mutant Ninja Turtles*, *Transformers*, and other brand products for children that are sold internationally through the collective efforts of films, TV commercials, and the toy industry. This hard-line commercialism could be one of the reasons why serious cultural critics and parents in Denmark were not drawn to the film, since we are not used to seeing a film as the center of such an all-encompassing campaign. However, it is precisely this concept that has characterized Disney and the Disney Corporation since the mid-1930s. This was the reason why Walt Disney, inspired among other things by the amusement park Tivoli in Copenhagen, and ignoring opposition among top Disney management, proceeded to create Disneyland in the Los Angeles suburb of Anaheim in 1955. Here, children would be able to participate and engage interactively in the fantasy worlds that Disney films provided for them.

The Danish newspapers dutifully participated in the promotion of *The Little Mermaid*. Since reviewers paid little attention to the financial aspects of the project, they offered two pieces of advice to readers: forget Andersen and enjoy the film as an impressive artistic experience in its own right. Both pieces of advice are rather beside the point. Although the fairy tale is quite radically reinterpreted, Disney nonetheless manages to express something Andersenian in the film version. And although the film is an impressive work of art in many respects, it has nonetheless been misunderstood as an appeal to both parents and their children.[3]

In the film, the little mermaid is transformed into a figure that is, from the beginning, more clearly related to the land than to the sea. In part, this is because the film depicts her in relation to the human, while the transcendental and religious dimensions of the fairy tale are absent. Also, the worldview and the devices used in the film clearly reflect the contemporary American cultural industry. The message of the fairy tale is conveyed in terms suitable for a modern public, but it is integrated as a component of a brand product that in many respects cheats its intended public of small children by making the daughter's emancipation from puberty into the turning point of the story along with the advice to parents to allow their children more freedom.

Like other Disney productions, this film invokes a series of stories alongside the text of the fairy tale. These are not joined together into a single well-balanced story, but instead remain like loose fragments that are not appreciated on their own but are experienced as free-floating, malleable quotations. If they point towards anything collectively, it must be the filmmaker's – or our own – expectations about postmodernity. It is open to discussion, then, whether the film represents a new tradition that fulfills in a real sense the Romantic period's expectations regarding the free work of art, or whether it merely reproduces our confusion. If the film was meant to help dissolve the "placelessness" of children in the media age, it could have taken these children as its starting point instead of merely handing them sporadic momentary experiences. As is customary in the media industry, Disney usually gift-wraps its product in sexuality in a form of "Freudian Lite." Even this is not done consistently, however, since the sexual element is toned down in the film version of the story. Any family can happily go and buy a Happy Meal at McDonald's afterwards. Who thinks of the ox that made the hamburger as they munch?

In Denmark, the film was not on the circuit for long, whereas it became a genuine success in the US precisely because it gave American girls an opportunity to continue playing the mermaid. A line of mermaid costumes was launched after the film, and the Walt Disney group produced a sequel with the subtitle, "Return to the Sea" (Kammerud and Smith 2000). In this sequel, the mermaid and the prince are now married, and we follow their daughter, Melody, who is drawn to the sea without understanding the danger represented by the sea witch, Morgana. If Morgana gets hold of Melody, she will gain control over the seven seas.

The Mermaid as Icon

An icon is a picture, a statue, or, more specifically, an image of a saint. A distinction is made between the (made) object that signifies and the person, object, or idea that is signified. It is a question of a special form of comparison, between a canvas and a face, for instance, that also assumes a *tertium comparationis* for such a comparison to be possible. For example, in what ways does the two-dimensional, black-and-white picture resemble the three-dimensional, living face with its spectrum of colors? Broadly speaking, iconography deals with what pictures mean, in particular what portraits and statues mean as well as with the development of such motifs. In a more narrow sense, iconography deals with the attributes and symbols used to depict gods, heroes, and saints. As one sees, there are a number of similarities between the two definitions, and an analysis of "The Little Mermaid" quite easily spans both definitions. In the final section that follows, however, I refer to the narrower definition of iconography, since the figure of the little mermaid shares many features with the female saint.

Andersen's mermaid can be understood as a siren in reverse. Instead of seducing human beings, she wishes to live as one herself – she is seduced by them, in fact. At the same time, life as a human being is first and foremost a means to eternal life. She wishes, through love, to surpass finiteness and temporality and to achieve eternity. Human life is the platform that makes it possible to connect the animal and the divine. The *tertium comparationis* is love, which, when seen from an animal perspective, amounts to sexual drive and the loss of virginity/acquisition of guilt. From the perspective of the divine, it amounts to both self-sacrifice and good deeds. Seen in this way, the mermaid, with her seductive powers, is neither threatening to people nor is she seduced by them into becoming something foreign to her nature. She is already human, and in her bifurcated, half human-half animal body, she exhibits in humankind the split between the divine and the human. Søren Kierkegaard described Christianity as the belief in the absurd, in the paradox he calls "God-Man," or Jesus, who is the "God in Time" and who is found in the moment, the atom of eternity, in which temporality and eternity cross each other (1963, 6: 170–80).

The mermaid is not the messiah that Jesus is. After her childhood at the bottom of the sea, she desires to ascend – by virtue of her deeds at sea and on land – to the ethereal sphere in order to prepare, together with her sisters, for an eternal life as a saint. If she is a saint, she may well belong among the highest saints of the Catholic Church: those who were martyred for their faith. It is the martyrs, in particular, who, like the mermaid, have separated body from mind, and in the legends about them, descriptions of the instruments of their torture play an important role like that of the knife in Andersen's fairy tale. The text is, in any case, rather more Catholic than Kierkegaard would have appreciated. In his chief work on the interface between ethics and religion, *Kjærlighedens Gjerninger* (*Works of Love*, 1847), Kierkegaard opposes human love, which ascends like the mermaid to the earth's surface, to Christian love, which descends (1963, 12: 168). In John 3:13, a similar view of the spatial realities of human and divine love is expressed: "No one has ascended into heaven but he who descended from heaven, the Son of Man."

© *Translated by Stephanie Buus*

Notes

1. There is a difference between the manatee, which lives along the tropical coasts on both sides of the Atlantic and up the rivers, and the dugong, which lives in the ocean between India and Australia. A larger species, the Steller's sea cow, became extinct during the 1700s.
2. See Hauch's letter to Ludvig Bødtcher dated May 22, 1837 in Dal (1990, 6: 134ff).
3. It is only possible to summarize at this point the more general conclusions drawn from a detailed analysis of the film. For a complete analysis, see my article "Disneyfikation – den lille oversøiske havfrue" in *At se teksten. Essays om tekst og billede*. Odense: Odense Universitetsforlag, 1993.

References

Andersen, H. C. (1930). *Hans Andersen's Fairy Tales.* London: Ernest Nister.

Ariès, P. (1960; translated 1982). *Barndommens historie.* Copenhagen: Nyt Nordisk Forlag.

Barlby, F. (1994). *Det dobbelte liv. Om H. C. Andersen.* Copenhagen: Dråben.

Dal, E. (1990). *H. C. Andersens Eventyr,* vols. 6 and 7. Copenhagen: C. A. Reitzel.

Fausing, B. and P. Larsen, eds. (1980). *Visuel kommunikation,* vol. 1. Copenhagen: Medusa.

Kierkegaard, S. (1963, 3rd ed.). *Samlede Værke,* 20 vols. Copenhagen: Gyldendal.

Simonsen, I. (1942). *Den danske Børnebog i det 19. Aarhundrede.* Copenhagen: Nyt Nordisk Forlag.

Newspaper Sources

Fyens Stiftstidende and *Politiken,* 17 August 2003.

Filmography

Clements, R and J. Musker. (Directors) (1989). *The Little Mermaid.* US: Disney Studios.

Kammerud, J. and B. Smith. (Directors) (2000). *The Little Mermaid II: Return to the Sea.* US: Disney Studios.

THE EIFFEL TOWER:
CULTURAL ICON, CULTURAL INTERFACE

Stephanie A. Glaser

In July 2000 I surveyed forty-four primarily German and French students at the Universität des Saarlandes to find out what they knew about the Eiffel Tower.[1] Surprisingly, it was very little. Even if the question, "Who designed the Eiffel Tower?" might be considered misleading – since it was, in fact, not "Mr. Eiffel" as most conjectured – but two of his employees who drew up the original plan, the students' responses indicate much about the general perception of the tower. While most students had been there, few had bought souvenirs, considering them to be too expensive, too kitschy, or too touristy. A few admitted to buying postcards, stamps, key chains, or a miniature tower. Many admired the tower for the view, and some were impressed with its height; a few found the tower beautiful, but several of the French thought it ugly. More Germans than French commented upon its technical features, and regardless of nationality, almost all agreed that the tower is the national symbol of France because "everyone knows it," a response that confirms the tower's iconic status while actually ignoring the complexities of that status.

About the tower's origin students were less sure. Twelve students admitted ignorance, while three (all French) knew the exact date and reason for its construction. Most guessed that it had been built for "the universal exhibition" or "expo" sometime between 1813 and the early twentieth century, and a few came close to the exact date. Two thought the tower had something to do with America, confusing it with the Statue of Liberty, one suggested that it had been a gift to France from the United States. Most surprisingly, perhaps, a German student declared that the tower had nothing to do with French history and therefore was not the symbol of France but of mankind's achievement.

These responses suggest two important issues bearing on our understanding of cultural icons. First, the students' impressions – the view, the tower's height, its technical achievement, its beauty or ugliness, its universal character – echo ideas that were reiterated during its erection from 1887 to 1889. At three hundred meters, the tower was then the world's tallest building. Why then do these contemporary responses bear such striking similarity to those of the late nineteenth century? Is it because these qualities have become clichés that people now seek to experience for themselves? If so, does this indicate a continuity underlying the transmission of meaning? Or, is there something perennially unique about the tower and individual experience of it? More significant, however, is the lack of knowledge – demonstrated even by the French students – about the actual circumstances relating to the tower's creation and construction. This ignorance is possibly a sign of its cultural embeddedness, which points to the silent or concealed historical and cultural layers that, unbeknownst and probably unimportant to the modern viewer or consumer, have contributed to its present meaning. The iconic status of the tower might therefore be understood as the result of a process of accumulating meaning, obfuscating on one hand the object's original significance (which may, however, persist in some latent form), and, on the other, continually transforming its subsequent meanings.

In its very substance, then, the cultural icon engenders a dialogue between present and past. It serves as an interface: as a link and as a boundary. As a link, it opens a window to the past that can be partially recaptured by tracing continuity in tradition or meaning; as a boundary, however, it impedes this vision, for both the loss of meaning that occurs as the object attains iconic status and the range of loose associations that are substituted for the lost significance create an object disconnected from historical reality, as illustrated by the German student's perception. This comes very close to what Gérard Farasse wrote of the tower, using a metaphor that gives insight into this phenomenon: "In the child's mind the Eiffel Tower is not a cultural object but a natural object that lies outside of history. It has always existed and will continue to exist just like the sky, the rocks, and the trees. It was not created at a specific moment."[2]

The ahistorical character of the tower corresponds to its symbolic status in the popular imagination. Rich in meanings at its construction for the Universal Exposition of 1889, the tower was intended to be a memorial of the French Revolution, a monument to progress and human (i.e., French) achievement, a symbol of social solidarity, a spectacle at which the world should marvel, an amusement for the citizens of the Third Republic; for its detractors it signified the ugly triumph of capitalism and industry. Its modern meaning pales in comparison with these grand ideological dimensions. Now standing out as the symbol of Paris, it has assumed all the clichés associated with the city: love, perfume, fashion, champagne, beautiful women, or, viewed sardonically, "la légèreté française" (Farasse 1990: 97). Its original and pointed meanings have been replaced by generalities. Our current understanding of the tower is thus founded not only upon a rupture with the past, but upon a real dichotomy between the particular and the seemingly universal.

My purpose in discussing the tower as a cultural icon is to recover the cultural, historical, and ideological context in which it came into being and then to trace the processes by which it attained its present meaning, and, in so doing, pick up threads of continuity between its original use and significance and our present conception of it. Visual and verbal works will be taken as documents reinforcing the meanings that have been imposed upon the tower over time. The primary issues are to determine at what point the original meanings lost their force, what physical circumstances imposed new meanings, and what media then codified these in the popular imagination. Thus, after having begun with my students' twenty-first-century interpretation, I turn to the past to reinstate the Eiffel Tower in its original setting, moving from there to the twentieth century to explore its ensuing meanings in connection with historical and ideological factors. Finally, I shall analyze in what ways the current iconic significance of the tower relates to its past meanings.

Before beginning, however, it is necessary to set forth the particularities of the tower as cultural icon. Unlike personalities like Madonna or Nelson Mandela, or a work of "high art" such as the *Mona Lisa*, Edvard Munch's *The Scream*, or Edward Hopper's *Nighthawks*, the Eiffel Tower is a work of architecture, an engineering feat that was public and "popular" from the beginning, becoming a subject of high art only in the twentieth century. We are not dealing with the same kind of "popularization" or "degeneration" of an image in the public mind as with the aforementioned artworks. Moreover, because symbolic and nationalistic meanings were imposed upon it even before its completion, its iconic status has always been related to, as well as confused with, its function as a national symbol. Most importantly, the tower appeared at a decisive historical moment. Engendered by the emerging industrial society, its meanings were constructed by that society and its spin-offs: consumerism, public transport, mechanical reproduction, print culture. These combined in the creation of the tourist industry, with which, now as then, the tower is closely connected.

Cultural Embeddedness: The Eiffel Tower in the Nineteenth-Century Architectural Context

In his 1900 *Conférence sur la tour de 300 mètres* Gustave Eiffel (1996: 73–124) placed the tower as the culmination of a series of architectural ventures. The first project for a cast-iron tower attaining the symbolic height of 1,000 feet (304.80 m) was drawn up by the English engineer Richard Trevithick in 1833 to celebrate the vote on the third Reform Bill in 1832 (Lemoine 1989a: 79), an act that transformed the parliamentary system of representation in favor of the working classes. Though never undertaken, the project was resuscitated in 1874 by the American engineers Clarke and Reeves, who proposed to build a 1,000-foot iron tower to commemorate the American Revolution for the centennial celebration coinciding with the Universal Exposition in Philadelphia in 1876. The tower would highlight the progress of science and art through the centuries (Lemoine 1989b: 21). Although praised in the pages of *Scientific American* as an eminently national construction because of its material and its commemorative significance (Eiffel 1996: 121), the American tower nonetheless shared the same fate as the English one. Both projects anticipated Eiffel in their use of iron to reach never-before-attained heights and in their grand ideological significance: symbolizing the triumph of a new social order, commemorating the freedom assured by democratic government, and celebrating the progress of the sciences and arts.

Although iron was a relatively new building material, stone was still being used in the construction of tall buildings. Cologne Cathedral, completed in 1880, was the highest building in the world, its spires rising to 157.38 meters (Wolff 1990: 50). In light of the Prussian defeat of the French a decade earlier, it could likely have appeared as the very image of German power and might. Five years later, however, the Washington Monument, a granite obelisk of 169 meters, exceeded the cathedral in height.[3] In 1884 Jules Bourdais, architect, and Amédée Sébillot, engineer, inspired by the 1,000-foot towers, proposed to build a 300-meter granite tower that was to serve as a monumental lighthouse illuminating Paris. This project would compete against Eiffel's and the other 105 plans submitted to the 300-meter tower competition opened in 1886 by Edouard Lockroy, *Ministre du commerce* and *Commissaire général* of the forthcoming Universal Exposition (Lemoine 1989b: 22–23, 33–35).[4]

Thus the idea for a 300-meter tower was in the air. In 1884, anticipating the Universal Exposition and the centennial of the French Revolution, two of Eiffel's engineers, Maurice Koechlin and Emile Nouguier, drew up the plan for a commemorative tower, whose form was derived from that of the pylons used to support the viaducts and bridges produced by Eiffel's company, primarily those of the Garabit Viaduct (1879–1884) on which Koechlin had worked since his entry into the company in 1879 (Lemoine 1989a: 57, 86). These pylons were in themselves supreme engineering feats, the result of meticulous calculations that increased their sturdiness and resistance to wind, designed and perfected by Eiffel and his engineers. The same structure, designed by Koechlin, had been used for the internal support of the Statue of Liberty (Lemoine 1989a: 74). Bereft of its functional status, the pylon that became the Eiffel Tower highlights the particular form and design that characterized Eiffel's many engineering projects. Its simple skeleton was dressed up by architect Stephen Sauvestre, who added decorative arches below the first and second platforms, a glass arcade on the first platform, statues of trumpeting angels on the second, and an immense glass bulb at the top (Lemoine 1989b: 26–29). Though simplified in its final form, this plan won Eiffel's support. Publicizing it in the 1884 *Salon d'automne*; publishing the plans in *Le Génie civil*; presenting it before the *Société des ingénieurs civils*; and discussing the tower's scientific benefits with experts in weather, astronomy, and physics, Eiffel emphasized that the tower was a product and consequence of the Enlightenment and the French Revolution, both of which, he emphasized, had prepared the way for the triumph of art and science in the nineteenth century (Lemoine 1989b: 29, 32–33), connecting it in size and ideology with its unachieved precedents.

In his 1884 design, *Projet de monument commemoratif à ériger à l'Exposition Universelle de 1889*, the tower is situated between the cathedral Notre-Dame de Paris and the Arc de Triomphe and rises four times higher than the cathedral. More than highlighting the tower's height, however, the monuments on either side of the tower highlight its principle characteristics: the Arc de Triomphe designates the tower's arch as a triumphal one, which Sauvestre had intended to serve as the gateway to the exposition (Lemoine 1989a: 86). More interesting is the connection between the tower and the cathedral's spire, completed by Eugène-Emmanuel Viollet-le-Duc twenty years earlier. Height had traditionally been the province of sacred architecture, with Strasbourg Cathedral's single spire being the highest point in Europe until Cologne Cathedral surpassed its 142 meters. Strasbourg's spire was one of the few to have survived the French Revolution, when spires were systematically torn down for insulting the principle of equality. In the nineteenth century these were re-erected, and restored medieval edifices and newly constructed neo-Gothic churches were crowned with spires. The spire had come to symbolize what the Revolution had made possible, social unity, and that which the nineteenth century sought to establish, concord between religious and civil powers (Leniaud 1987: 19, 29). Viollet-le-Duc (n.d., 3: 368) considered the church tower and spire to symbolize the industrial and commercial development of a city, or, in other words, progress in society. Spires also had a spiritual significance, representing the union between heaven and earth, God and man, as well as the ascension of the Christian soul in prayer (Leniaud 1993: 499). With the surge of religious feeling after the 1848 revolution, spire building became one of the important undertakings of the Second Empire (Chevalier 1997: 227). The tower might very well be seen as one consequence of this development.

Besides sharing form and symbolism, spires and the tower presented similar challenges to their constructors. Their "practically immaterial ascension" represented the superiority of man's knowledge and abilities over nature's forces (Leniaud 1987: 22, 1993: 499). Rebuilding spires was a feat that demanded technical expertise, required precise calculation, and an informed choice of materials; it also presented the challenge of working at great heights (Leniaud 1987: 22). The first neo-Gothic spire designed in nineteenth-century France was Rouen Cathedral's, constructed in cast iron by Jean-Antoine Alavoine in 1822 after lightning destroyed the preceding wooden one. Though much criticized, and completed only in 1884 (Desportes 1971: 58–59), Alavoine's pioneering venture anticipated Eiffel's in several ways: the tower was assembled from precast iron parts; it was designed not to imitate wood or stone, but to exploit and highlight the possibilities of iron and thereby bear testimony to the advances of science; it could be used to indicate the direction of the wind and provide a place for meteorological experiments; and, most importantly, it was to be the tallest structure in the world (Bideault 1979: 142–43; Desportes 1971: 51, 57–58; Leniaud 1987: 23; Murphy 1995: 205, n. 10).

Gustave Eiffel's Tower

The tower both culminated the century's developments in iron architecture and construction techniques and initiated a new era of building. It resulted from Eiffel's experience in designing and producing ever-lighter supporting iron structures, for unlike the supporting pylons from which it derived, the tower relied not on trellises for its stability, but on the positioning of the pillars and their convergence, which create points of resistance and direct the force of the weight (Lemoine 1989a: 88). Its four pillars absorb its entire weight, while the curve of the arches gives the impression that the 7,300-ton structure ascends weightlessly (Levin 1986: 44). Like Alavoine, Eiffel exploited what he saw as the potential of iron as a building material in order to erect an open, light, yet stable and resistant structure to never-before-attained heights. He exploited new technology like cranes and elevators and developed effective and secure means of working at great heights: scaffolding and lifts transported workers and materials. Moreover, innovative ways of illuminating the site and providing the elevated stations with power were found. Even laying the foundations required new skills and methods, and a new procedure for assembling prefabricated parts was initiated (Levin 1986: 44, 1989a: 1061, 1989b: 24).

Contemporary photographs, such as those by Edouard Durandelle, focused on the progress of the construction methods and techniques. Instead of focusing solely on the building process, however, Henri Rivière's photos captured the ambience of the construction site. They form a narrative that chronicles the life of the workers at the site: the photos show them at lunch or at rest, working from lifts and scaffolds, and in the company of the visiting industrialists or dignitaries. Often the images highlight the courage and daring required of those working on the Tower. Rivière adapted some of these photos in an album of lithographs, *Les Trente-six Vues de la Tour Eiffel* (1902), where the tower appears either close up and under construction or as a slender silhouette visible from different quarters of Paris. One of the most dramatic images, "En haut de la Tour" (Figure 3.1), shows four men at work on the tower, three of them on a wooden platform, which, attached to the huge iron frame, seems to hang precariously in the sky. The danger and drama of their position is highlighted by the absence of the Parisian landscape in the background, where instead darkened clouds seem to close in on the workers, giving the impression that the men are suspended and isolated in mid-air. Exposed to the elements, they work on despite the strong wind whipping the ropes of the scaffold, a detail that intensifies the sentiment of danger felt by the viewer. Similarly to Eiffel's concern for his workers and their working conditions, Rivière's evocation of the construction site can be understood in relation to the nineteenth-century's increasing concern for the working classes.

Eiffel saw the tower's construction as a community-building enterprise that forged worker solidarity. His dealings with the workers were forward-looking: skilled and unskilled workers were hired on the basis of merit, wages were set through a process of bargaining, and workmen acquired new skills on the site (Levin 1989a: 1055, 1058). This transformed the faceless laborer into an active and cooperating participant in a common goal. This vision was shared by the workers, who were enthusiastic about the project and proud of participating in such an endeavor (Cordat 1955: 113, 115).[5] Despite the physical demands placed on them, the workers were entirely committed to the finishing the project on time. To honor those working during the final, most strenuous and difficult stage of construction, Eiffel had their names inscribed on the tower (Levin 1986: 43, 1989a: 1058, 1989b: 23).

Although Eiffel declared that the tower's construction united the working force and industrialists in a common goal, this remained a utopian

Figure 3.1 Henri Rivière (1864–1951) Série des Paysages parisiens: en haut de la Tour Eiffel © RMN (Musée d'Orsay)/René-Gabriel Ojéda.

vision: at the festivities celebrating the tower's completion, a simple party was held for the workmen and a lavish banquet for the dignitaries (Levin 1986: 27). What is true, however, and what the government made much of, was that Eiffel's project had created an unprecedented network of workmen, suppliers, manufacturers, insurance agents, and lawyers (Levin 1989a: 1063, n. 2). It was also a commercial success, paying for itself almost immediately, and stimulating growth in the metallurgic sector. Most importantly, for Republican officials, the tower stood out as a monumental example of progress, which took shape with the aid of new technologies and the cooperation of all parties involved regardless of social class (Levin 1989a: 1061). For these reasons and others the tower may be seen to stand as a democratic monument par excellence.

The Universal Exposition of 1889

The early Third Republic coincided with a time of instability caused by economic crisis and deepening social tensions, which were linked to the increasing industrialization of what had been primarily an agrarian country. Though purported to ensure individual freedom and social equality, by the 1880s industrialization had resulted in dividing the working class, the main body of the Republic, into skilled and unskilled labor, and had further demarcated the working from the middle classes. For some Republican officials, this situation seemed to parallel the pre-Revolutionary system of privileges too closely and undermined the democratic principles upon which the Republic had been founded (Levin 1989a: 1056). Furthermore, they considered the devaluation of labor, another consequence of industrialization, incompatible with a Republican society in which freedom to work and to achieve solidarity through work were essential (Levin 1989b: 22). Consequently, Republican policy in the 1880s aimed to turn this tendency around and to give labor greater importance. The Universal Exposition of 1889 served as an expression of this policy, offering a model for the new social order resulting from new technologies and labor, which would, it was hoped, stimulate the necessary transformation within French society (Levin 1986: 42). The Eiffel Tower was the key monument in the realization of this program.

The exposition celebrated the centennial of the French Revolution by focusing on the progress made by the French since 1789. The official view was that by freeing labor, the Revolution had inaugurated a new social order and had permitted advances in science and art. In this ideological context, the tower stood as a direct consequence of the Revolution, demonstrating what a century of technological innovation could achieve. The connection between the tower and freedom comes to the fore in the engraving, *Gloire au centenaire* (Figure 3.2), in which six French flags

Figure 3.2 P. Clemençon. *Gloire au centenaire*. Engraving. © Collection Tour Eiffel. D. R.

fan out behind a Phrygian-capped Masonic triangle with the dates 1789 and 1889 running in parallel to its sloping sides. Below, an immense sun bursts forth from behind the bulky mass of the Bastille, symbol of the evils of the old order, which contrasts dramatically with the Eiffel Tower rising elegantly in front of it. To the right stands Gustave Eiffel, not attired in the suit of the industrialist but wearing a worker's smock. Leaning upon a mallet with which he has broken the huge prison chain lying at his feet, he stands with his left foot upon a royal staff in defiance of the old order, which has been vanquished by the new, represented by the engineer cum worker. The meaning is clear: the chains of bondage have been broken by the workman, and his creation, the tower, signals the triumph of the new order, as if out of the heavy iron chains the slender tower had been forged. Eiffel thus came to be seen as the embodiment of the democratic hero, "the entrepreneur who combined in one person the knowledge and skill of the craftsman and the initiative, daring, and imagination of the scientist, businessman, and artist" (Levin 1986: 42). He was the prototype of a new generation of builders and leaders of society, and his connection with the tower turned him into a sort of icon, which helps to explain why the tower bears his name.[6]

This image is fully in keeping with the ideological background of the exposition, which linked up topographically with the Revolution through the establishment of its major structures on the Champ-de-Mars, the vast field which had been leveled for the *fête de la Fédération* on 14 July 1790 and had served as place of assembly and celebration during the Revolution (Fauquet 1984: 75). The exposition also honored the revolutionary heritage by providing a place of community where visitors could share in the common experience of learning about new technologies and enjoying the peace and pleasure that labor had brought about (Levin 1986: 42, 1989b). While the Galerie des Machines and the Palais des Arts libéraux vaunted the industrial strength and modernity of France and manifested the progress in science and the arts through educational displays and exhibits of inventions (Levin 1986: 25), the Eiffel Tower, situated directly opposite the Galerie des Machines at the other end of the Champ-de-Mars, provided the monumental gateway to the exposition and served as a microcosm of the grand plan.

According to Edouard Lockroy, the tower represented the cooperation between government and business (Levin 1986: 42–43, 1989b: 23); it also allowed the public to participate in the experience of new technologies through the elevator rides and staircases and to enjoy the pleasure of viewing the panorama of Paris, shopping, or dining in the restaurants on the first platform. Most importantly, however, the platforms and stairways of the Eiffel Tower would serve to create a community, where people from every social class as well as all parts of the world would cross paths

(Levin 1986: 42, 1989b: 24). Lockroy insisted that the tower's very structure symbolized the makeup of a democratic society: "its many small parts, each clearly articulated and composed of the same material, each reduced to its most efficient form and interlocked with the others to form an integrated, controlled dynamic system" (Levin 1986: 44, 1989a: 1058, 1989b: 23). Thus, in its intricately connected parts, the tower offered an image of the Republic where individuals worked together for the common good.

Lockroy also claimed that the tower was the visible manifestation of progress, for "it summarized the industrial greatness and power of the present age. Its immense shaft, by burying itself in the clouds, had something symbolic about it; it seems the image of progress as we conceive of it today: an unending spiral in which humanity gravitates in an eternal ascension" Levin (1986: 45).[7] This conception of an upward spiraling movement of humanity towards an ideal social order underlay Jules Michelet's 1851 project for a Republican altar, a monument of the people, where the *grands hommes* who had prepared and brought about the Revolution would be placed in concentric circles rising to the enthroned maternal image of France (Fauquet 1984: 75–76, 78). Connecting the spiraling progress of humanity with eternal ascension, Lockroy used the language of neo-Christianity, which, as Paul Bénichou explained (1977: 71–73), understood salvation in terms of Revolutionary ideals, as the collective redemption of society through progress, liberty, and fraternity. Lockroy correspondingly linked the tower with the cathedral spire, making the former stand out as the symbol of social solidarity and progress, turning it into a new sacred structure – the sign of industrial strength and of the forward movement of humanity towards a new and perfected social order.

It is difficult to measure the public's understanding of the exposition's grand educative program and of its ideological importance. For engineers and industrialists the tower was a symbol of technical knowledge and national prestige, whereas for the general public it was a diverting attraction (Levin 1989b: 27). Enjoying its renewed liberty granted by the Republican government, the press played an important role in promoting the tower, following its construction and publicizing its progress in photos and in reports, such as the *Figaro* article describing a typical working day at the construction site (Cordat 1955: 106–15). Such publicity made people inhabiting even remote regions of France eager to visit the tower (Levin 1989b: 24). This enthusiasm continued through the exposition, on whose guide books' covers the tower figured prominently. For the middle- and upper-class public, the newspaper *Le Figaro* published a daily called *Figaro de la Tour*, printed at their office in the tower (Lemoine 1989b: 70; Ory 1989: 44). Most popular imagery focused on how the masses perceived the exposition, with the tower figuring consistently in the background. For example, *La Caricature* saluted the opening of the exposition on its title page where the arches of the Eiffel Tower provide the background to a scene in which, amid a crowd of foreign passers-by, a Parisian woman helps two primates wearing suits and hats to orient themselves with a map.[8] This satiric commentary on the exposition presents the tower fulfilling one of its projected roles as a place where the inhabitants of various lands come together.

The tower also figured in advertising posters, which had become a widespread means of communication (Levin 1989b: 16–17). In a railway advertisement for the Paris-Lyon-Méditerranée line's 25 percent reduction on tickets to Paris for the opening of the exposition, the tower stands prominently underneath the white lettering "Exposition Universelle de Paris 1889" (Figure 3.3). The combination of the tower and the railway is significant, for both were products of new technologies and stood out as symbols of modernity; moreover it reflected social reality, for the railway was becoming a popular means of transport – many visitors would have made the journey to the exposition by train. Here, the combination of new printing techniques, the role of advertising, and the germinating idea of tourist travel combine to make this poster an image of modernity as celebrated by the exposition.

The overwhelming presence of the Eiffel Tower in popular imagery and in the paintings of now little-known artists contrasts with its absence in "high art," excepting Georges Seurat's 1889 pointillist painting of the structure nearing completion and Douanier Rousseau's 1890 self-portrait with the tower, *Moi-même, portrait paysage*. This absence can be explained by the vehement criticism with which Eiffel's project was greeted by many artists and intellectuals. In 1886 Charles Garnier, Guy de Maupassant, and Charles Gounod signed the *Protestation des Artistes*, which condemned the "inutile et monstrueuse tour Eiffel" as insulting the artistic heritage of France: "une gigantesque et noire cheminée d'usine, écrasant de sa masse barbare Notre-Dame, la Sainte-Chapelle" (Eiffel 1996: 61–64). A century earlier, Notre-Dame de Paris and the Sainte-Chapelle had been described as "barbaric masses," despised signs of injustice and tyranny; by 1889, however, they represented beauty and architectural accomplishment. An oft-repeated anecdote is Maupassant lunching at the Eiffel Tower because it was the only place he could go in Paris without having to look at it (Barthes 1989: 7). Whether detested or marveled at, the tower was an inescapable presence in Paris and became part of everyone's life. Surprisingly these negative responses had petered out by 1900, when the tower had become passé and stone had once again become the preferred material for monumental architecture. It would remain for the twentieth century to create an enduring image of the Eiffel Tower and bestow upon it its international significance.

Figure 3.3 Robert Delaunay. *Red Eiffel Tower (La Tour rouge)*. 1911–12. Oil on canvas, 49 $\frac{1}{4}$ × 35 $\frac{3}{8}$ inches (125 × 90.3 cm). New York: Solomon R. Guggenheim Museum. © The Solomon R. Guggenheim Foundation, New York. 46–1036.

Cultural Icon: The Eiffel Tower in the Popular Imagination of 1900

By the turn of the century, the Republican ideology that had been used to promote the Eiffel Tower had failed: the condition of the working classes had not improved, class conflict had increased, and economic competition had stiffened. Consequently, the clearly delineated ideological plan of the 1889 Exposition found no equivalent in the 1900 Exposition, for instead of educating the visitors and lauding the benefits of progress, the exposition seemed to glorify the leisurely life with dramatic electrical effects (Levin 1989b: 35).[9] Though magnificently illuminated by electric lights for the 1900 Exposition, the tower received half as many visitors as it had in 1889, testifying to the waning enthusiasm for it.[10]

The image of the tower, however, changed with the development of the postcard. Some of the first cards, called "Libonis" after Louis-Charles Libonis, who designed them, were printed in the *Figaro* office at the tower during the 1889 Exposition with images of the tower and were sold as souvenirs (Jenger 1989: 9). By 1900 the postcard had become a commercial enterprise whose success was assured by the 1900 Exposition, for which a vast number of cards featuring panoramic views of Paris that included the Eiffel Tower, were produced (Jenger 1989: 17). These cards appear to reflect an early identification of the tower with Paris in France and abroad.

The Eiffel Tower and the Nation

According to the original contract, the tower and the other buildings erected for the 1889 Exposition were scheduled to be demolished in 1909. Though the tower was being used by Eiffel as a laboratory, its role as a telegraph station ultimately saved it. In 1898 a telegraph line had been installed between the tower and the Pantheon, and in 1903 the French army installed a wireless telegraph, which by 1912 could contact every sector of the globe (Lemoine 1989b: 76–81).

After 1914 the tower became a national symbol, when its telegraph station intercepted intelligence about a German attack on the Marne, which the French army was then able to prevent off (Lemoine 1989b: 81). The tower thus proved to be a key strategic instrument, which explains why Hitler (who had himself photographed with the tower) took it over in World War II, using it to transmit information and entertainment to his troops. During the Occupation, a banner was draped under the tower's second platform declaring "Deutschland siegt auf allen Fronten," – a reference not only to the physical siege of Paris, but also to Nazi control of the invisible yet all-permeating radio waves.

Above the banner an immense "V" heralds the imminent victory of the Nazi forces (Lemoine 1989b: 89). The Nazi takeover of the tower contributed to intensifying its connection with the capital – in contemporary images it symbolized French resistance and infused the city's motto, "Fluctuat nec mergitur," with greater meaning. On a more light-hearted note, a cartoon depicting 25 August 1944 shows Charles de Gaulle striding down the Champs Elyseés towards an open-armed female Eiffel Tower that exclaims "Mon Grand!" Here the Eiffel Tower, now returned to the French, represents Paris liberated (Des Cars and Caracalla 1989: 79, 80, 84).

The Eiffel Tower in the Arts

In the era preceding World War I, avant-garde artists and writers consecrated the tower as the emblem of modernity, symbolizing the break with traditional forms of visual and verbal representation and offering a new means of perceiving the world. Endeavoring to paint the immense and intricate structure that seemed to resist representation altogether, Robert Delaunay rendered the tower simultaneously from several points of view, crunching it and compacting it into the picture frame in his Eiffel Tower paintings of 1910 to 1911 (Figure 3.3). In 1913, Blaise Cendrars transferred the concept of visual simultaneity to a written text, creating the first "livre simultané," *La Prose du Transsibérien et de la Petite Jehanne de France*, in which his text shares the page with Sonia Delaunay's paintings (Cendrars 1996: 3–11). The latter capture the verbal rhythms of the text of this "poème-Train" (Bonnefis 1990: 161), a personal and transcontinental voyage that terminates visually and verbally with the Eiffel Tower, its red form complemented across the page by the closing verse: "Paris Ville de la Tour unique du grand Gibet et de la Roue" (Cendrars 1996: 11). In bringing the railway and the tower together, Cendrars associates the tower with dynamic movement and turns it into the symbol of the fusion of spatial dislocations.

This coalescence of time and space also underlies Guillaume Apollinaire's 1913 poem "Zone", which conflates ancient and modern eras and Eastern and Western traditions under the aegis of the tower, evoked as a kind of deity at the poem's opening (Apollinaire 1990: 7). This vision of the tower can in part be understood in light of its use as a telegraph station connecting all parts of the world. Another poem written during the war, "2e canonnier conducteur" combines this view with nationalistic sentiments in the verse shaped like the tower, "Salut monde dont je suis la langue éloquente que sa bouche O Paris tire et tirera toujours aux Allemands" (Apollinaire 1965: 214). This passage is preceded by a verse shaped like Notre-Dame de Paris, "Souvenirs de Paris avant la guerre ils

seront bein plus doux après la victoire" (Apollinaire 1958: 72). Symbols
of the nation, the monuments symbolize French resistance – the cathedral through memory, the tower speaking to the world and defying the
enemy. A more vivid representation of the tower's telegraphic activity
comes to the fore in "Lettre-Océan," where groups of letters, words, and
verses radiate outward in concentric circles to form radio waves around
two distinct points: the phrases "Sur la rive gauche devant le pont d'Iéna"
and "Haute de 300 mètres" (Apollinaire 1958: 36, 37). Rejecting the
instantly recognizable silhouette that would reinforce the tower's status
as object, Apollinaire represents the tower as "Haute de 300 mètres",
with this phrase as the central point around which the letters circle. This
representation turns the tower into an agent, highlighting its activity and
its dynamism, while underlining the poem's theme of oral and written
transcontinental communication. Here, the tower's function in fusing the
spatial and temporal might be understood as a reworking or an extension
of the original idea that it served to bring people together.

The premise of the tower's modernity was overturned in Jean Cocteau's
1921 play *Les Mariés de la Tour Eiffel*, which takes place on 14 July to
ironically commemorate the French Revolution by underscoring the
banality of the modern world and of the French middle classes, the heirs
of the Republic. Evoking the dichotomy between the tower's original
status and its use as telegraph station: "She was queen of Paris. Now she's
a telegraph girl,"[11] Cocteau uses the tower as a vehicle for societal critique. In contrast, Robert Delaunay's paintings of the 1920s highlight the
tower's monumental character. Unlike the early paintings in which the
raw, metallic structure had signaled the tower's modernity, the later works
focus on its sheer height, its huge pillars shooting upward in magnificent
colors (Düchting 1994: 64).

The fascination with movement and new points of view had already
been exploited in film with the Lumière brothers' *Panorama pendant
l'ascension de la Tour Eiffel* (1898) and Charles Pathé's 1900 film of the
tower from a moving walkway (Stiévenard 1990: 46). By the 1920s the
tower had become the setting for films such as René Clair's *Paris qui
dort* (1923) and Julien Duvivier's *Mystère de la Tour Eiffel* (1927), and
after mid-century it was a stock image for the *Nouvelle Vague*: François
Truffaut's *Quatre Cent Coups* (1960) opens and closes with shots of the
Eiffel Tower. A decade earlier, Hollywood had confirmed the connection
between the Eiffel Tower and Paris for American audiences in films such
as Vincente Minnelli's *An American in Paris* (1951) or *Gigi* (1958),
where the tower was a necessary presence, serving no narrative function
except to mark Paris as the location. According to director Billy Wilder,
a bottle of champagne and the tower became necessary features of any
cinematographic creation of a Parisian scene (Stiévenard 1990: 51);

moreover, the tower was used as a balcony for romantic encounters until Hollywood directors transferred these associations to the Empire State Building (David 1990: 61–62), as in Leo McCarey's 1957 *An Affair to Remember*. However, Lawrence Kasdan's 1995 *French Kiss* demonstrated that the tower has not lost its power to suggest romance. Reviving the trope of the Eiffel Tower as romantic balcony, this film is constructed around the cliché of Paris as the city of love; in this, the tower renews one of its original meanings as a meeting place for people of different backgrounds.

Cultural Interface: Disjunction and Continuity

Although the idea of the Eiffel Tower as a site of romantic encounter seems far removed from its status as a commemorative monument, when it is remembered that the French Revolution aspired to create a unified social body and that in 1889 the tower was intended to help bring about this hoped-for solidarity, it becomes clear that, fundamentally, the unifying power of the tower has remained intact, though it has been transferred from a grand social and political scale to the individual, private sphere. Yet, there is a larger community that the tower binds together in the present (Levin 1989b: 12). The idea of a community formed through commercialization, consumerism, visual culture, and the tourist industry has its roots in the nineteenth century, when the aristocratic grand tour as educational experience gave way to "tourism," as a middle-class "leisure" activity (Culler 1982: 129–30).

The rise of the railway also contributed to the spread and popularity of the religious pilgrimage, which can be viewed as a brand of tourism that resembled what could be called the "cult" of the Eiffel Tower. While the pilgrimage had traditionally been an arduous journey on foot with trials to overcome along the way, in the latter part of the nineteenth century, boosted by special-price tickets like those advertised in the PLM poster (Figure 3.4), it became a mass phenomenon that turned small places like Lourdes into busy centers with thousands of pilgrims visiting per year (Caron 1985: 111–13). Likewise, people came in droves to the Universal Exposition to witness the miracle of technology first hand. Like pilgrims, the tower's visitors participated in "a common ritualistic experience" (Levin 1989b: 26), yet they were able to do what even the most devoted pilgrim could only wish for – to take home part of the miracle. In 1889, miniature Eiffel Tower souvenirs were made of iron scraps from the construction site (Buisine 1990: 80; Levin 1989b: 26), relics of the tower of which they were consubstantial.

For many critics, including Barthes (1989: 21), the tower achieved its universal meaning through its reproductions. Alain Buisine (1990: 80)

Figure 3.4 © Musée Carnavalet/Roget-Viollet/Inauguration de l'Exposition Universelle de 1889. Chemins de fer Paris-Lyon-Méditerranée. Paris, musée Carnavalet.

asserts that its meaning is incomplete without them: "What is remarkable in the case of the Eiffel Tower is that its endless reproduction does in no way mean its betrayal, its degradation, its devaluation, but, on the contrary, its achievement, its totalization, its assumption."[12] This can be compared to Jonathan Culler's (1982: 132) view that "the proliferation of reproductions is what makes something an original, the real thing." Through its many reproductions, the tower is an object "toujours déjà connue" (Farasse 1990: 92), "always already familiar", which means that the visitor goes there to see in reality the image in his or her mind's eye, a conflation of the myriad reproductions he or she knows. This, coupled with the phenomenon of reproduction, has resulted in Eiffel Tower replicas being constructed in places as unlikely as Tokyo, England, the American Midwest, and Las Vegas, though none of them are life size. Though culturally and historically decontextualized, such replicas bear the mark of authenticity because they look like the original and offer a similar experience.

As a student, I was at the Eiffel Tower for Bastille Day in 1989, not because I knew about the Champ-de-Mars and its Revolutionary use, nor about Eiffel and his technical prowess, nor about the 1889 Exposition and the Republican program, but because it was going to be a fantastic party with lights, fireworks, and music. Unbeknownst to me and probably to many of the other thousands of people present, we were participating in a "common ritualistic experience." Through its existence the tower has been a focal point and place of celebration: stupefying visitors to the 1889 Exposition with a display of gas lighting and electricity, completely outlined in 1900 with electric lights, advertising "Citroën" in illuminated letters down its sides from 1925 to 1937, spectacularly metamorphosing under the colored lights and fireworks designed by André Granet for the 1937 Exposition, bearing the calendar counting down to the new millennium (as in Figure 3.5), and offering a spectacular cascade of water and laser lights to greet the year 2000. At every celebration, visitors renew the experience of these celebrations as well as the Revolutionary ones, and thus the tower serves as an interface, a space where the present and the past come together, fusing into a ritual moment. Yet the presence of the past in the modern understanding and use of the tower has been obstructed by its mediatization, and so the tower also acts as an impediment to such fusion.

A recent image of the tower that appeared on the cover of the German university magazine *Aud!max* highlights the issue's theme of vacation and travel (Figure 3.5). In the foreground a lightly tanned couple, laughing and obviously possessed by the "travel fever" the issue discusses, pose in front of a slightly askew tower. Through its arches, an equestrian statue, parked cars, streetlights, and pedestrians can be seen, with

Figure 3.5 Cover of *Aud!max. Die Hochschulzeitschrift*. April 2001. Courtesy of the *Aud!max* editorial board.

the Tour Montparnasse in the distance, indicating that the photo is a montage intended to send one message: the couple in Paris are having the time of their life. The image works on two levels: signifying Paris and, by extension, travel, leisure, pleasure – the "up and away" written on the bottom left of the cover, as well as being in Paris with your girlfriend or boyfriend, not in April as the song goes, but in high summer, as the calendar indicates (151 days left until the year 2000, which puts the couple in Paris in high summer at the end of July). Far removed in style and content from the nineteenth-century images, this photograph invokes our contemporary associations of the tower: travel, love, and Paris.

Conclusion

Such contemporary representations – whether those with a particular agenda, or architectural pastiches like at the hotel Paris Las Vegas, or the most common postcard photographs – make the tower a monument that is always up to date, and in so doing deny that it is a product of historical circumstance, an expression of nineteenth-century ideas about architecture and society, commemorative monuments, and building practices, whose meaning has been transformed and shaped over time by external factors. By reinstating the tower in its original historical and ideological context, this study has demonstrated how its significance at a given time was generated and reinforced by visual and verbal works propagated in official and popular discourses. It has shown that the Republican ideology that buckled after the 1889 Exposition permitted a small object, the postcard, to transform the tower from an ideal social and political monument to the internationally known symbol of Paris. Thereafter equated with Paris in poetry and the arts of the early twentieth century, during war the tower became the symbol of Paris and French resistance to foreign occupation. When Hollywood created its version of Paris in the 1950s, romance became an essential element of the Eiffel Tower = Paris equation.

These important moments of change in the tower's meaning enable us to draw the threads of continuity between our present conception and its past significance. Associated with travel and tourism from its origins, it designated the 1889 Exposition as a destination, whereas after 1900 it stood for Paris as the tourist's goal, and has now become a generalized marker for travel. In connection with the railway it stood out as a symbol of modernity: in the nineteenth century both were the newest and most forward-looking technological inventions, while in the twentieth century the tower was associated with dynamic movement and simultaneous vision that fused separate spatial and temporal realms. Finally, conceived as part of the Republican program to bring people together in a common experience, the tower was supposed to enable unity and social solidarity (which its role as a telegraph station broadened), a theme taken up by the avant-garde, who placed the tower as the omphalos of a new global vision. Today its unifying power has not lost sway, especially through its cinematic image as a meeting place for lovers. Ultimately, the tower has become part and parcel of our consumer culture. Though our contemporary view of it is far removed from that of the nineteenth century, the continuity in meaning and tradition reveals that as a cultural icon it is not only a product of rupture, but of a strange and surprising resonance between its original and accumulated meanings. Like other cultural icons, the tower engenders a dialogue with the past, inviting us to unearth its history and glimpse some of its former significance even as its present status might occlude these earlier meanings.[13]

Notes

1. Of the forty-four undergraduate and graduate translation students surveyed, eleven came from France, twenty-seven from Germany, and one each from Luxembourg, Scotland, Ireland, Finland, Russia, and Benin.
2. "Pour l'imaginaire enfantin, la Tour Eiffel n'est pas un object culturel mais un object naturel, hors histoire. Elle existe depuis toujours et ne cessera d'exister à la façon du ciel, des roches, des arbres. Elle n'est pas née à un moment donné du temps" (Farasse 1990: 91–92). Unless indicated, translations from the French are my own.
3. Though begun in 1848, the Washington Monument was not inaugurated until 1887, after work was abandoned from 1854 to 1877 because it was leaning (Eiffel 1996: 79–80).
4. Bourdais had designed the Palais du Trocadero for the 1878 Universal Exposition. In 1871 Sébillot had conceived a 300-meter iron lighthouse for Paris (Eiffel 1996: 74; Lemoine 1989b: 23).
5. Only two strikes had occurred during the twenty-six months of building (Cordat 1955: 115).
6. When he arrived in Paris in 1710, Eiffel's ancestor, Boenickhausen, added "Eiffel" to his name, after the Eifel region from which he came. After the Franco-Prussian war the family dropped Boenickhausen in favor of the more "French-sounding" Eiffel to avoid being suspected of collaborating with the enemy.
7. In her book, Levin includes both the original and the above-quoted English translation. Here she quotes from Lockroy's preface to Monod's *Exposition universelle de 1889* (xxv): "il résumait la grandeur et la puissance industrielle du temps présent. Sa flèche immense, en s'enfonçant dans les nuages, avait quelque chose de symbolique; elle paraissait l'image du progrès tel que nous le concevons aujourd'hui: spirale démesurée où l'humanité gravite dans cette ascension éternelle."
8. The front page of the 11 May 1889 edition of *La Caricature* bore this text: "Bienvenu aux étrangers. Venez, entrez, donnez-vous la peine de voir et d'admirer. Guidés par leurs interprètes, ils circulent . . . autour de la Tour, les touristes de l'Afrique du Sud, les indigènes de Bornéo, les rastaquoères de Papouasie, les citoyens de l'Australie centrale. On a même signalé déjà quelques gentlemen primitifs des îles de la Sonde, venus en garçons et logés par les soins de l'Administration au Jardin des Plantes."

9. This difference is best illustrated by the reuse of the Galerie des Machines: in 1889 it had housed the newest technological inventions, whereas in 1900 it was used to display food (Durant 1994: 5, n. 4).

10. 1,024,897 visitors in 1900 compared to 1,953,122 in 1889 (Lemoine 1989b: 65, 74).

11. "Elle était reine de Paris. Maintenant elle est demoiselle du télégraphe" (Cocteau 1993: 85).

12. "Ce qui est remarquable dans le cas de la tour Eiffel, c'est que son infinie reproduction ne constitue nullement sa trahison, sa dégradation, sa dévaluation, mais tout au contraire sa réalisation, sa totalisation, son assomption."

13. My sincere thanks go to Nils Holger Petersen and The Danish National Research Foundation for their generous support of this project.

References

Apollinaire, G. (1958). *Calligrammes*. Paris: Gallimard. (Orig. pub. 1918.)

———. (1965). 2e canonnier conducteur, dans *Œuvres poétiques*, préface d'André Billy, édition établie par Michel Adéma et Michel Décaudin. Paris: Gallimard, coll.

———. (1990). *Alcools*. Paris: Gallimard. (Orig. pub. 1913.)

Barthes, R. (1989). *La Tour Eiffel*. Paris: Centre National de la Photographie/Seuil. (Orig. pub. 1964.)

Bénichou, P. (1977). *Le Temps des Prophètes: Doctrines de l'âge romantique*. Paris: Gallimard.

Bideault, M. (1979). La flèche de la cathédrale de Rouen, par Alavoine. In *Le "gothique" retrouvé avant Viollet-le-Duc*. Paris: Caisse National des Monuments Historiques et des Sites.

Bonnefis, P. (1990). L'hyperbole de la Tour dans l'oeuvre de Blaise Cendrars. *Revue des Sciences Humaines* 218: 153–86.

Buisine, A. (1990). Le miroir aux photographes. *Revue des Sciences Humaines*, 218: 67–83.

Caron, F. (1985). *La France des patriotes de 1851 à 1918*. Paris: Fayard.

Cendrars, M. (1996). *Blaise Cendrars. L'or d'un poète*. Paris: Gallimard.

Chevalier, M. (1997). *La France des cathédrales du IVe au XXe siècle*. Rennes: Ouest-France.

Cocteau, J. (1993). *Les Mariés de la Tour Eiffel*. Paris: Gallimard. (Orig. pub. 1921.)

Cordat, C. (1955). *La Tour Eiffel*. Paris: Editions de minuit.

Culler, J. (1982). Semiotics of Tourism. *American Journal of Semiotics* 1(1–2): 127–40.

David, S. (1990). La Tour Eiffel au cinéma. *Revue des Sciences Humaines* 218: 61–62.

Des Cars, J. and J.-P. Caracalla. (1989). *La Tour Eiffel: un siècle d'audace et de génie*. Paris: Denoël.

Desportes, J.-P. (1971). Alavoine et la flèche de la cathédrale de Rouen. *Revue de l'art* 13: 48–62.

Düchting, H. (1994). *Robert and Sonia Delauney: the triumph of color*. Köln: Benedikt Taschen.

Durant, S. (1994). *Le Palais des Machines*. London: Phaidon.

Eiffel, G. (1996). *L'Architecture métallique*. Paris: Maisonneuve et Larose.

Farasse, G. (1990). La Tour Eiffel expliquée aux enfants. *Revue des Sciences Humaines* 218: 91–102.

Fauquet, E. (1984). J. Michelet et l'histoire de l'architecture républicaine. *Gazette des Beaux-Arts* 53: 71–79.

Jenger, J. (1989). *Souvenirs de la Tour Eiffel*. Paris: Réunion des musées nationaux.

Lemoine, B. (1989a). *Gustave Eiffel*. Paris: Hazan.

———. (1989b). *La Tour de Monsieur Eiffel*. Paris: Gallimard.

Leniaud, J.-M. (1987). Les flèches au XIXe siècle. In *Le Mont Saint-Michel, l'archange, la flèche*. Paris : Caisse Nationale des Monuments Historiques et des Sites.

Leniaud, J.-M. (1993). *Les Cathédrales au XIXe siècle*. Paris: Economica.
Levin, M. (1986). *Republican Art and Ideology in Late Nineteenth-Century France*. Ann
    Arbor: University of Michigan.
———. (1989a). The Eiffel Tower Revisited. *The French Review* 62(6): 1052–64.
———. (1989b). *When the Eiffel Tower was New: French Visions of Progress at the Centennial
    of the Revolution*. Amherst: University of Massachusetts.
Murphy, K. (1995). Restoring Rouen: The Politics of Preservation in July Monarchy France.
    Word and Image 2(2): 196–206.
Ory, P. (1989). *L'Expo Universelle*. Bruxelles: Complexe.
Rivière, H. (1989). *Les trente-six vues de la Tour Eiffel*. Paris: P. Sers. (Orig. pub. 1902.)
Stiévenard, J. (1990). Les 'Ecoles de la Tour'. *Revue des Sciences Humaines* 218: 41–59.
Viollet-le-Duc, E.-E. (n.d.) *Dictionnaire Raisonné de l'architecture française du XIe au
    XVIe siècle*. Paris: Librairies-imprimeries réunies.
Wolff, A. (1990). *Das Kölner Dom Lese- und Bilderbuch*. Cologne: Verlag Kölner Dom.

Filmography

Clair, R. (1923). *Paris qui dort*. USA: Films Diamant.
Duvivier, J. (1927). *Mystère de la Tour Eiffel*. France: Le Film d'Art.
Kasdan, L. (1995). *French Kiss*. USA: Polygram Filmed Entertainment.
McCarey, L. (1957). *An Affair to Remember*. USA: Jerry Wald Productions.
Minnelli, V. (1951). *An American in Paris*. USA: Metro-Goldwyn-Mayer.
———. (1958). *Gigi*. USA: Metro-Goldwyn-Mayer.
Truffaut, F. (1960). *Quatre Cent Coups*. France: Les Films du Carrosse.

EDVARD MUNCH'S *THE SCREAM* AS CULTURAL ICON

Hans Lund

Early in the morning on Saturday, 12 February 1994, two men put up a ladder against the National Gallery in University Street, Oslo. One of them climbed up, smashed the windowpane, and climbed inside. A moment later he threw Edvard Munch's famous painting *The Scream* down to his accomplice. A surveillance camera opposite videoed the ninety-second robbery. That morning the attention and expectations of Norwegians were turned in quite another direction, since a few hours later the greatest media event in Norwegian history was to take place, the opening of the Sixteenth Olympic Winter Games at Lillehammer. This sensational art heist competed strongly with the inauguration of the Olympics in the evening papers and TV news. The images captured by the surveillance camera were transmitted worldwide. On 9 May, the undamaged painting turned up again after a police investigation containing all the ingredients of a TV thriller.

The events surrounding the theft became motifs much used by newspaper cartoonists, such as burglars carrying the reluctant and screaming figure away from the gallery. The Austrian newspaper, *Der Standard*, depicted one of the burglars covering the mouth of the painted figure to muffle the scream. In a Norwegian drawing one of the gallery attendants is turned into a scream figure when he discovers the burglary, while another shows the director of the gallery turned into the prominent scream figure when he is informed of the ransom of 8 million Norwegian crowns. And, when the painting was finally back safely in the gallery, a Norwegian newspaper showed the scream figure with a big smile triumphantly raising its arms, beaming with joy.

85

For at least half a century, *The Scream* led a double life on and beyond the National Gallery. After the burglary the picture was established more than ever as the favorite of the mass media and popular culture. It appears in comics, it is used by the advertising business, it supports information campaigns of different kinds; in the papers it frequently comments on topical political events. It directs its scream to a wide and heterogeneous target group, addressing not only those interested in art, but also those who are not in the habit of visiting museums.

One may ask what are the qualities or characteristics of *The Scream* that make this work so attractive and useful to popular culture. What is there in the picture that established itself as a cultural icon? Within the popular cultural sphere *The Scream* is of course not read in the same way as within the institution of art. As a work of art the picture represents a psychological and existential trauma deeply rooted in the radical aesthetics of the period around 1900. What happens, then, with *The Scream* when the picture is adopted by popular culture? This question is discussed below.

The Picture

During the last fifty years *The Scream* has come to be identified as Edvard Munch's most famous painting. The painting in the National Gallery in Oslo (1893) is not Munch's only version of *The Scream*. Another important painted version (1893) is exhibited in the Munch Museum in Oslo. The most reproduced version is probably the lithographic one (1895). Turned towards the observer of the picture, a thin, bald figure stands screaming near a safety railing. Deep below the railing is a fiord, stretching into a city. Waving bands of clouds blaze over the sky. In the painted versions the bands are red. The bald figure with the open mouth has the form of a long, narrow, curving sack. The sex of the figure is indeterminate. The road and railing cut in a steep diagonal up towards the left corner. Furthest away in the road two little dark men in top hats are moving away from the central figure. The road and the railing, in contrast, seem to be rushing towards the observer. "Contemporary studies on the psychological content of lines identify descending lines as generating an unhappy or sad mood" (Heller 1973: 117). According to Heller, Munch took the diagonal from Van Gogh's pictorial world, where it serves as "a formula for death." The motif becomes reversed when Munch transforms his pictures from painting to engraving. The only exception is *The Scream*, where the graphic version keeps the direction of movement from the painting, something that indicates that the diagonal movement down towards the right corner in this case was of great importance to the artist.

What is the story behind the picture? Munch confirms that the figure at the railing is screaming. The picture is often understood as an expressionistic representation of the individual's isolated and disturbing confrontation with that which she or he does not understand. Interpreters have discussed mental trauma, an encounter on the abyss of emptiness, chronic anxiety, or what the Germans call *Lebensangst*. The sweeping lines in the sky support such a reading of the picture. It is possible to interpret them as sound waves as well as indicating a feeling of dizziness. The parallel vertical lines to the right in the graphic version and the heavy red color with its conventional symbolic meaning also point in such a direction. There is hardly any other picture before the turn of the eighteenth century that in such a genuine way recreates the experience and condition of existential human anxiety.

Sometimes the painting is entitled *The Scream on the Bridge*. Thus the Swedish poet Werner Aspenström opens his ekphrastic poem "The Scream" with the following: "The scream floats in rings over the water/and the abutments of the bridge shake as at the spring flood" (Aspenström 2000: 9, translation H. Lund). The railing in the painting might possibly be perceived as a bridge. If so, the bridge is improbably high with a dizzy perspective over the city and the water. The site of the motif has actually been located on the road that winds up towards Ekeberg in Oslo and from which there is a splendid view over the city and Oslo fiord. The church steeple that can be clearly observed in the lithographic version of the motif borrows its form from the Frogner church that even today can be seen clearly from the site of Munch's image.

On 22 January 1892 Munch wrote a memorandum in his diary:

> I walked along the road with two friends – and the sun went down. The sky suddenly became blood – and I felt like a breath of sadness. I stopped – leant against the railing dead tired. Over the bluish-black fiord and city Clouds of dripping steaming blood were lying. My friends walked on and I was left Behind in anxiety with an open wound in my breast [And I felt then there went] a big scream through nature. (Heller 1973: 106)

Munch reported that usually he didn't paint what he sees, but what he has seen. Under one of the signed prints of the graphic version of *The Scream*, Munch quotes in German from his own diary: "Ich fühlte das grosse Geschrei durch die Natur" (Heller 1973: 88). For that reason it is reasonable to interpret *The Scream* as an illustration of, or a comment on, the text from the diary and, accordingly, as an autobiographical document. However, the picture does not tell a story: it does not really describe an external scene, rather it represents a state of mind.

In Munch's private library, in the Munch Museum in Oslo, is found the 1923 edition of Søren Kierkegaard's *Collected Works*. One of the very few volumes of this omnibus work whose pages were cut by Munch is the volume that contains, among other things, *The Concept of Anxiety* (*Begrebet Angst*). In his work Kierkegaard distinguishes between fear and anxiety. Fear signifies unpleasant feeling of external threat. Anxiety, on the other hand, is the dreadful feeling of internal threat. This internal threat is what Munch seems to represent in his picture: "There is less fear of an external event or thing which would cause harm than there is anxiety resulting from turning inward, from self-contemplation . . . . Anxiety and dread are projected from the interior to the exterior" (Heller 1973: 68).

Just as the child is born with a scream, so was the twentieth century. *The Scream* became an emblem for the deep anxiety that the new century brought. Oskar Kokoschka mentions the picture in terms of world anxiety (*Weltangst*), whereas Arnold Künzli sees the picture as an expression for anxiety as the disease of the Western world: *Angst als abendländische Krankheit*. Herman Bahr speaks of the picture as the scream that introduces expressionism and the new century (Zaloscer 1985: 14).

Stereotype, Paraphrase, and Icon

When *The Scream* was brought into focus at the exhibition *Echoes of the Scream* at the Arken, Copenhagen, spring 2001, it was by virtue of the fact that this picture is a key work of art of the nineteenth century, a work that, with its signs of apocalyptic anxiety, had a deep impression on art over the last century. Echoes of Munch's painting can be found in Artaud's dramas, in some of Egon Schiele's self-portraits, in Pablo Picasso's *Guernica*, in Francis Bacon's roaring pope and also in one of Pink Floyd's album sleeves.

The Scream still appears as the stereotypical face of anxiety. "In the great blooming, buzzing confusion of the outer world we pick out what our culture has already defined for us, and we tend to perceive that which we have picked out in the form stereotyped for us by our culture" (Lippman 1993: 134). Richard Dyer (1977) distinguishes between *typing* and *stereotyping*. Without the use of types, it would be difficult, of not impossible, to make sense of the world. The world is understood by referring individual objects, people, or events in our heads to the general classificatory schemes into which they fit. The stereotype, on the other hand, takes as starting-point a few simple, easily comprehensible and recognizable characteristics: "stereotyping reduces, essentializes and fixes 'difference' . . . . It then excludes or expels everything which does not fit, which is different" (Hall 1997: 258).

It is natural that works of art that have become common stereotypes for one phenomenon or another will also be the subject of *paraphrasing*. The paraphrase plays on the fact that the observer recognizes the picture to which the paraphrase alludes; the source text can be located in the target text – or using Gérard Genette's terms, the hypertext can be located in the hypotext (Genette 1997: xv). Consequently, the paraphrase presupposes that the observer remembers the picture to which the paraphrase refers, that he or she notices resemblances and differences. *Stereotype* and *cultural icon* are not identical phenomena. The stereotype locks the picture to a specific reading, while the cultural icon is flexible and adjusts itself to different contexts. Accordingly it can be given different meanings.

For over one hundred years *The Scream* has been regarded as a stereotype for anxiety and fear. But recently the picture has been primarily paraphrased into the world of cultural icons. *The Scream* is given new meanings through popular cultural adaptation and rewriting. Rewriting is, according to Matei Calinescu (1997: 243), "a relatively new and fashionable term for a number of very old techniques of literary composition." A number of key concepts in poetics can be assembled under this umbrella concept: imitation, parody, burlesque, transposition, pastiche, adaptation, and also translation. Calinescu discusses literary texts, but the term *rewriting* can of course also be used in the study of the visual arts. When certain well-known images are subject to repeated rewriting and put into new contexts, it may be due, among other things, to the fact that it is often easier for the designer to borrow an idea for an image than to create a new one. "Designers are under pressure of time to fulfill their design briefs . . . and it is therefore easier to borrow images than to create them from scratch. Use of familiar images facilitates rapid communication and permits parody" (Walker 1994: 66).

Word and Image

The strength of the image "is to detach a moment from its temporal sequence and make it hang there in perpetual non-present representational present, without past or future" (Miller 1992: 66). However, the person who looks at the image seldom has the opportunity to give this power his or her undivided attention. More often than not a verbal text appears, intruding into the semantic territory of the image. And quite often the text loads the image with a kind of time sequence.

As mentioned earlier, Munch has quoted from his own diary, below the graphic version of *The Scream*, a caption that completes the meaning that the title gives to the picture. Many years ago a visitor to the National Gallery in Oslo wrote in small letters directly on the canvas: "Can only have been painted by a mad man." This was, of course, an act of sabotage, but at the same time one cannot disregard the fact that the text affects the observer standing in front of the painting. The graphic images are susceptible to verbal interference. An alternative title can easily change the meaning of the image. Titles like "Yawn," "Cry," or "Song" might possibly have invited different readings: "A work differently titled will always be aesthetically different" (Levinson 1985: 29). In other words, the title is an integral part of the work. It is, according to Jerrold Levinson, always aesthetically relevant. "Titles are names which function as guides to interpretation" (Hollander in Fischer 1984: 288). Not all titles function in the same way, however. Levinson distinguishes between core content, i.e., the meaning of the work without a title, and the meaning that the work derives with a title applied to it. Starting from this distinction he establishes a typology of different title categories and their influence on the core content. Two of his categories are of interest here. One of them he calls "neutral titles." They add very little to the picture and they principally repeat what can already be understood from the core content. They are redundant. Levinson names another category, "undermining" or "opposing titles." The undermining titles "are titles whose ostensible drift is counter to that which they crown, and which oppose the work's provisional statement with a statement tending in a contrary direction." Levinson further states: "Some of these titles within the undermining category play on irony, turning the meaning of the core content upside down." Levinson illustrates this point by using Peter Blume's painting *The Eternal City*, showing Mussolini's Rome in ruins. Other types of undermining titles are not ironic, Levinson writes, "but instead persist in their contrariness, yielding effects of humor, shock, or anxiety . . . . Non-ironic undermining titles thus generate work contents quite different from the core contents they subsume, if not quite the reverse of them" (Levinson 1985: 35).

The cultural icon is normally based on a verbal text. This is especially true of well-known pictorial works that have been transposed into new contexts such as advertisements or cartoons, or that have been paraphrased into such contexts. These texts are often of the type that Levinson calls undermining. The reader's attitude is dictated not only by the genre – the advertisement demands a response different from the reader than does the cartoon – but also by the context. "The context provided by the *Daily Telegraph* is very different from that provided by the *Socialist Worker* . . . . Readership and reader expectation form part of this context" (Storey 1993: 86). The titles or short texts that accompany the popular cultural rewritings of Munch's picture are mostly examples of the title category that Levinson calls undermining. *The Scream*, the title that Munch assigned his picture is, in its redundancy, an example of what Levinson calls "neutral titles." The title's redundancy and the fact that the picture creates a condition rather than an event make *The Scream* easily affected by captions assigned to the picture. For example, in 1996 it was the fiftieth anniversary of Munch's death and, according to Australian law, copyright expired with regard to the use of Munch's pictures. The *Sydney Morning Herald* celebrated with a competition. Well aware that captions added to pictures change their meaning and that the cartoon genre requires a specific reading strategy, readers were invited to generate captions for *The Scream*. One of the proposals received changed the scream figure into a frustrated mother: "but Mummy I want an ice cream why can't I have an ice cream please can I have an ice cream Mummy."

The Cartoon Category

In the introduction to a book of jokes on modern art that accompanied an exhibition of the same theme at the Tate Gallery in 1973, George Melly (1977: 9) writes: "Running parallel to the public reaction, the cartoonists of each era have left behind them a humorous graph of the impact of various phases of modern art . . . . The body of the cartoons took as their subject matter those movements and, more particularly, those individual pictures or sculptures in front of which the public reacted most violently." Melly illustrates his point using Manet's *Olympia* and Matisse's *La Dance*. Munch's works are not mentioned. Today it would hardly be possible to avoid including the Norwegian painter in such a volume, not least *The Scream*. Already in 1895 a couple of Oslo's comic magazines published caricatures of *The Scream* in connection with an art exhibition. During the last four decades, especially after the 1994 burglary, cartoonists have constantly drawn on *The Scream*. We see the scream figure bellowing at the parking meter, or being comforted by children offering empathic questions. We see it screaming with horror when firemen carry it out of a museum in flames.

In a German cartoon the scream figure is dressed in a skirt posing for an artist. A mouse runs over the floor of the studio and the female model screams. The artist exclaims: "Ja! Bleib so! Das ist gut!" (Yes! Do not move! That's good!) In *The New Yorker* (1983) a number of people are sitting in a library absorbed in books; on two signs we read "Silence" and "Quiet." A man who is standing at the art history shelf drops a heavy folio onto his foot. A balloon above his grimacing face indicates, however, that he is suppressing his scream. He compensates by imagining Munch's scream figure at the railing.

Comic Strips

Munch's horrified figure is not infrequently seen in comic strips. It has appeared in, among others, *Mutts*, *The Buckets*, and *Dylan Dog*. A typical example is Bill Holbrook's comic strip *On the Fastrack* (1987), where a woman looks for a picture to hang in the corridor of her place of work. "Nothing seems to express the true spirit of the company," she complains. She can find only abstract and pastoral pictures. Finally, however, she finds a suitable picture: Munch's *The Scream*.

The Scream has also inspired absurd strips. In *Cowboy Henk* by Kama & Seele, popular in the Netherlands, published in *NRC Handelsblad* (Amsterdam), a bald man with huge ears visits Henk, who at the time is a hairdresser. Henk cuts his ears off and the customer leaves the hairdressing salon. Outside in the street some liquid spurts out of the ear holes and the man is turned into Munch's scream figure. The story is told without any verbal text.

In *The New Yorker* (1990), headlined "Munch in Manhattan," the scream figure is sitting in a restaurant. The waiter welcomes him while the figure is screaming. In the following image the figure studies the menu with a satisfied expression. The waiter recommends a fish dish. The scream figure is screaming. In the following picture the scream figure is eating in peace and quiet. The waiter appears again, offering pepper for the salad. The scream figure is screaming. In the last picture but one there is peace at the table. The waiter is again standing beside his guest, asking: "Everything all right, sir?" The scream figure is screaming. This comic can be read in two different ways. One can understand the screams as the guest's way of calling the waiter, or one can interpret the screams as the guest's frightened reaction to the waiter's words. In the first case the comic becomes "normal," in the second case it becomes absurd.

Commercial Advertising

In his book *Art in the Age of Mass Media*, John A. Walker argues that there are

> countless magazine adverts and TV commercials that employ works of art as props. Their role is to serve as tokens of high culture, superlative skill and supreme value, and to signify the good taste, the sophisticated lifestyle of the human beings appearing in the adverts. The product or service being advertised is supposed to acquire these qualities by association or contiguity. (1994: 51)

Of course this is correct, but at the same time we must not forget the many cases where rewriting results in a humorous contrasting picture. For instance, the women in Jean François Millet's painting *The Gleaners* appeared some years ago in an advertisement with golf clubs in their hands instead of sheaves of corn.

According to BONO (Billedkunst. Opphavsrett i Norge [Pictorial Art Copyright in Norway]), the authority that oversees the rights both of art museums and heirs of artists, Munch's *The Scream* is much coveted by advertising agencies. BONO receives about one thousand applications annually for the use of *The Scream* in different connections. *The Scream* is, above all, much used in the American advertising world, whereas it is rarely appropriated in Europe. In Europe, copyright for works of art is valid for seventy years after the death of the artist, while in the US only for fifty. Currently, few restrictions limit the use of *The Scream* in the US as long as the companies keep the advertising within the American continent. In Europe, permission would need to be applied for, and BONO is reluctant to give permission for advertisements that in any way ridicule the picture or connect it with dubious contexts. Applications from Coca-Cola, McDonald's, and Levis have been rejected, as has an application from Sony to use *The Scream* to publicize Michael Jackson. For purely ethical reasons the pharmaceutical industry has been generally denied permission to use *The Scream*.

In 1996 the London Underground launched a poster campaign with the headline "Think what you save when you buy a ticket." In the rectangular poster we see through a coach window the backs of a female and a male passenger and their reflection in the opposite row of windows. The reflection in the windows shows the two people from the front: while the woman is reading a book in peace and quiet, the reflection of the man shows Munch's well-known anxiety-ridden face. The reflection of the man does not correspond with his figure from the back. What we see – with the help of the caption – is not what the man looks like, but how he feels. He feels like the scream figure. Evidently he hasn't bought a ticket!

In the US the scream figure appeared in an animated commercial for 1997 Pontiac cars. It stands screaming in the road when Pontiac's red sports car turns up and stops. The scream figure jumps into the car and drives away happily.

Press Drawings

The Scream has frequently been linked with political issues and social problems. The biggest category of all is press drawings commenting on political, social, and cultural topics. The fact that the use of *The Scream* in this rewriting category is so much more extensive than in advertising may have to do with the fact that this sector has in practice become a free zone. The Munch Museum does not react in a negative way to this category of press drawings: "When it comes to press drawings and other political satire, used as editorial material, we choose not to react," it has been stated on behalf of the museum (Hoff 1993).

When Queen Elizabeth II expressed her famous "annus horribilis" in December 1992, she appeared in the papers as a scream figure with her crown on her head. In 1984, after the American presidential election and the British parliamentary election, *The Scream* appeared in the *Observer*. The two background figures in their top hats commented on the scream in the foreground of the picture: "It's the thought of Reagan and Thatcher until 1988." Similar fears were expressed in a picture, spread in the press as well as on T-shirts before the American presidential election in 1988: "Your worst nightmare: President Quayle." Quayle, who was notorious for his clumsy public statements, was vice-president under George Bush. He had announced himself as a presidential candidate when Bush's term was coming to an end.

Financial politics have been constantly commented on by means of *The Scream*. Munch's figure has appeared with the dome of the American Congress building as headgear, and a large number of politicians have taken on the role of the scream figure. In American and Swedish cartoons taxpayers have also been given the part of *The Scream* when it was time for readers to send in their income tax returns. In the Wellington *PSA Journal* in 1987, Munch's figure stands frustrated in front of a billboard with the words: "Rationalisation! Layoffs! Corporatisation! Evisceration, Restructuring, Reorganisation! Sackings! Redeployment, Redundancy, Severance!"

Social phenomena such as stress, shopping crowds, fixation on cosmetics, racism, and lack of academic independence have been commented on in the European and American press by means of *The Scream*. The threat of nuclear weapons was linked to Munch's picture in the *Minneapolis Star and Tribune* in 1983 and in the newspaper *Verdens Gang* (Oslo) in 1995. The terror attack against the Pan Am plane over Lockerbie was depicted by a paraphrase on *The Scream* in the *Irish Times* (1988). Cultural politics are also often reflected in the newspapers by means of *The Scream*. After the reduction of the subsidies to culture by the American Congress in 1995, *New York Newsday* put the scream figure in front of the Congress building with the letters NEA (National Endowment for the Arts) written in white on his black shirt. Two years later, in the *Charlotte Observer*, a man with a bow-tie puts his question with authority to the scream figure sitting beside him, "Must you react like that every time we Republicans cut the NEA?" In the spring of 2000 the Dutch Minister of Culture reduced subsidies to the Dutch academies of art. In the *NRC Handelsblad* (Amsterdam) a drawing was published representing the minister lying naked on a couch with a tiny lyre in his hands. An electric heater standing in front of the couch illustrates the hard cultural climate, and the lack of strength is illustrated by the minister's diminutive penis. On an easel beside the couch Munch's well-known figure is screaming.

Posters, Kitsch, and Urban Context

The Scream has been used frequently in connection with information and propaganda campaigns of different kinds. An effective poster campaign against smoking was conducted in the Netherlands in 1997. Munch's screaming face was paraphrased in the shape of white smoke rings on a dark background. The text was short: "Roken. Dood – & doodzonde," which means: "To smoke, to die – that would be a pity."

On 24 January 1996, Shell Oil hosted a reception at the Phillips Collection in Washington, DC. At the same time, outside the museum building, a demonstration against Shell's cooperation with the Nigerian military dictatorship occurred. While the reception and the demonstration were taking place, two Greenpeace activists fastened a big banner to the front of the building. It showed the scream figure together with the caption: "Stop Shell in Nigeria." On another occasion Greenpeace introduced a poster depicting the harpooning of a whale. The scene is a whaling boat; the harpooner is standing at the prow. The figure is standing at the rail. In front of the boat the fiord in Munch's picture is transformed into a white whale.

In a Republican poster campaign against President Clinton's plans for national medical service reform we see a fictitious plastic card showing the seal of the United States and the words "Health Security" and "United States of America." The card stretches towards the interior of the picture like the road and the crash barrier in Munch's *The Scream*. Aggressive zigzag lines run across the card, which is surrounded by fire. In front of the card the scream figure is standing with its hands to its temples. Under the picture it says in capital letters: "Health care. Oh Noooo!" Then follows in smaller letters: "The public grows fearful of Clinton's plan and shows little faith in alternatives. Is reform doomed this year?"

Munch lived for many years in a house in Pilestredet Street in Oslo. When in 1990 the authorities decided to demolish the house, architectural students protested. They painted a huge and almost exact copy of the lithograph *The Scream* on the gable of the house. Under the picture they wrote the words "No to demolition. The School of Architecture." The building is still there, uninhabited, but with the picture intact. The huge Munch copy has become a well-known pictorial element in the center of Oslo. The Munch Museum and BONO have not protested against the students' rescue action. Bass Taverns, one of Great Britain's biggest pub chains, has established thirty-three *It's-a-Scream* pubs (it-makes-you-scream-with-laughter pubs) all over Great Britain. The signs outside the pubs show *The Scream*, and inside there are allusions to the picture, among other things in a pattern of holes on the lamps. The Scream pub in York has been located at Monkgate (the pronunciation of the word monk in Norwegian, munk, is equal to the pronunciation of Edvard Munch's name). For the marketing of the pubs the owners produce among other things T-shirts and yellow bags with text in black: "It's a Scream," and of course they have established their own website. The world of *The Scream* kitsch has grown rather extensive. The image has appeared on key chains, ties, mouse pads, posters, bookmarks, coffee mugs, and spoon rests. The most famous object is probably the inflatable doll produced in the US.

Internet and Film

When one uses Internet search terms like "Scream," "Schrei," and "Cri," it becomes apparent that Munch's picture is very well established in the world in both commercial and private contexts. The picture is also used in other connections, for instance, as a welcoming picture on the website for psychological advice to students at Indiana University, Bloomington, labeled *Angst Central* and *Angst Café*.

Much of the scream material on the Internet is American. Of course this material also reaches Europe, where it should legally fall under the copyright rules of the European Union. But BONO's insufficient resources limit the measures it can take against use and abuse. Moreover, it has been suggested that too many interventions might in the long run harm Munch's reputation.

Around the turn of millennium many websites advertised the feature films *Scream, Scream 2*, and *Scream 3* (1996–2000) by the American director Wes Craven. The *Scream* films belong to the so-called slasher genre, a category of horror film where a serial killer chooses his victims from frightened teenagers. The film trilogy, especially *Scream*, are known for their many and often ironic references to other horror films. With their continual intertexts, their self-referentiality, and their play with the genre expectations of the audience, they stand out as well-crafted genre parodies.

A survey of *Scream* and *Scream 2* reveals that the references to Munch's picture concern only the face of the scream figure and not other parts of the film. The little murderer, who is wearing a *Scream*-like mask, moves silently and quickly around in the film. It is the murderer's victims who are screaming, not the murderer himself. It is the murderer who is continually rushing, not the road, as in Munch's picture. In the painting it is the screaming figure that seems to be struck with horror, in the film the murderer in his mask and a black, monk-like cowl arouses horror in others (Haastrup 1999: 2, 21–28).

The murder mask in the *Scream* films almost immediately found its way into the American and later also into the European Halloween celebrations. The good-natured pumpkin with its open, shining mouth has a rival and a counterpart in the pale, long and narrow face with its mouth wide open, surrounded by a black hood. After 1997 it could be bought in shops selling Halloween decorations. By this contribution the paraphrase of *The Scream* seems to be even further removed from its origin. The scream mask is to the general public what Jean Baudrillard (Mirzoeff 1999: 28) calls *simulacrum*, i.e., a copy without an original, a copy existing in many places but where no "original" can be shown.

In the spring of 2000 the Bank of Scotland advertised the SonyCard in British newspapers. In the advertisement is a face of a young man with his mouth open, who seems to be screaming. Across his face runs the word "Scream" in big, white letters. To the left above this word is written, in smaller type, "It makes you," and below to the right is written "laugh, or cry." "Scream" and possibly the diagonal in the layout of the text might refer to Munch's *The Scream*, but probably not many of those who read advertisement would register such an intertext. Most young people would probably form associations with the film *Scream* or with the British pub chain – Munch, who is he? It should also be observed that the word *scream* has a double meaning in English. It is not only an expression for "a loud, high-pitched piercing cry expressing fear, pain, extreme fright," but also for something positive, namely "an irresistibly funny occurrence or person" (Thompson 1995).

Carnival

Many of the examples of paraphrase and rewriting of *The Scream* recall what Mikhail Bakhtin (1969: 35) calls the carnival. The purpose of medieval carnivals was to conquer the fear both of the spiritual and the profane power that characterized everyday life in a controlled way, to ridicule the authorities with their threats and injustices through ritual carnival laughter. The carnival brought a victory "über die Furcht vor allem Geheiligten und Verbotenen (vor dem "Mana" und vor dem "Tabu"), vor der Macht Gottes und vor der Macht der Menschen, vor den autoritären Geboten und Verboten, vor Tod und Vergeltung im Jenseits, vor der Hölle, vor allem, was entsetzlicher ist als die Erde" ("over the fear of what's holy and forbidden [of 'Mana' and of 'Taboo'], of God's power and of men's power, of authoritarian decrees and prohibitions, of death and retaliation in life to come, of hell, of everything more terrible than earth.") (Bachtin 1969: 35). For a short period, the world was upside-down. John Docker (1994: 185) points out that "carnivalesque as a cultural mode still strongly influences twentieth-century mass culture, in Hollywood films, popular literary genres, television, music." When popular culture turns *The Scream* upside-down it is of course not with the same existential overtones as when the carnival turned upside-down the explicable and inexplicable threats of everyday life. It is rather an expression of a new era's playful way of dissociating itself from leaders, canonical verbal and visual documents, and stereotyped truths. Peter Brookner (1999: 23) is correct when he says that the carnival idea can be applied only "metaphorically or by extension to other activities in discussion of contemporary popular culture." In any case, it is evident that there are certain similarities between carnival culture and parts of popular culture. "It is never enough to speak of popular culture, we have always to acknowledge that with which it is being contrasted" (Storey 1993: 18). Nicolas Mirzoeff (1999: 11) points out that "'art' has become the oppressive Other for cultural studies that allows popular culture to define itself as popular."

The adaptation of *The Scream* is in many ways characterized precisely by the Other. Fear replaces anxiety. While Munch's picture, which shows the scream figure's inward condition projected on the pictorial space as a whole, can be seen as a representation of anxiety in the spirit of Kierkegaard, in popular culture representations of the anxiety-ridden figure it is changed into a fearful figure possessed by an external threat, e.g., by the two black figures in the background, or as in the *Scream* films, into a figure that itself infuses horror.

But popular culture can also give us a counterpart in which we see a satisfied, happy and laughing scream figure. In a cartoon by the Norwegian artist Finn Graff we see the figure in its frame on the wall burst out laughing at the sight of two bizarre female museum visitors. An article in *Dagbladet* (Oslo) in 1991, entitled "Norwegian Self-confidence," is illustrated by a scream figure with a brilliant white smile. In a Norwegian advertising folder for video recorders we see in a comic strip the disappointment of a family experiencing a visit from some relatives who invited themselves, which obstructs the evening's episode of *Falcon Crest* on TV. On the wall is seen Munch's framed figure yelling out its disappointment. In the last picture is the denouement of the drama. The wife says goodbye to the guests and the husband rushes up to the video they had just bought. On the wall the figure is laughing happily.

The pictures on our walls are silent. So is *The Scream* as well. But in the world of popular cultural paraphrase, the emphasis lies only on the latent or real sound emitted by the painting. We have seen examples of this earlier: the man in the reading-room who drops a book on his foot or the burglar who holds his hand in front of the screaming mouth on the canvas. A cartoon in *The Herald-Times* (Indiana) in April 2000 shows the painting at a museum flanked by two loudspeakers. A man presses a button beside the picture over which is written: "Now with surround-sound." In January 1991 *The Journal of Art* published a drawing in which some museum visitors with earphones for guiding are making faces in front of *The Scream* because of the terrible sound. Paraphrases of the picture have been used in the debate on the sound environment. *Frankfurter Allgemeine Zeitung* showed in 1987 a picture on its first page representing the scream figure surrounded by a radio, a dripping water tap and a table fan. *The Daily Telegraph* (1994) used the picture as an illustration for an article on muzak, the monotonous background music played in shops. The big color illustration shows the scream figure surrounded by notes and billowing lines. One of the popular cultural paraphrases that has attracted most attention was published in *Time* (1998) as the core picture for an article on tinnitus. The figure is at the railing with its mouth closed with the forefinger of its right hand resting on its lips. Under the picture is written in large white capitals: "Shhh . . . ." The attention focused on the picture was caused not only by the ingenious and amusing design of the paraphrase but also about the fact that *Time* had not asked for permission from the Munch Museum. Since *Time* is also sold in Europe, the magazine is bound by the copyright rules of Norway.

A third category of counterpart in the paraphrasing of Munch's picture concerns the gender determination of the scream figure. Is it a man or a woman? The Australian Barry Humphries, the creator of Dame Edna, maintains that the painting represents a woman. *The Scream* "is a painting of a woman at sunset who has lost her earrings." In one of his TV programs Dame Edna acted as a scream figure dressed in a hand-painted, hair-raisingly vulgar dress filled with scream figures. The Norwegian daily *Bergens Arbeiderblad* (1992) lets a female scream figure at the railing lift her skirt for the two gentlemen in the background – in order to illustrate the "prostitution" of Munch's pictorial world in popular culture. As already seen, the scream figure dressed in a skirt can refer to an antiquated caricature of a woman's fear of a mouse that is running over the floor. The female scream figure can also, however, appear in more serious connections. On the cover of *Nursing Mirror* (1983) the scream figure represents a female nurse. Around her the road and the railing are burning. The text below the picture refers to an article on hospital fires inside the periodical: "Could you cope in a blaze?"

Conclusion

As a work of art Edvard Munch's *The Scream* is part of our global cultural heritage. For over nearly a century the picture has been the foremost emblem for man's feeling of anxiety. The central position of this work in the era of reproduction has resulted in an increasing number of contrasting pictorial counterparts in popular culture. By rewriting and paraphrasing *The Scream*, by adding verbal texts, and by linking the picture repeatedly to new contexts and target groups, it has been possible to adapt the scream concept to new meanings.

In connection with an exhibition of Munch's graphic works in the Art Gallery of Ontario (AGO) in Toronto in the spring of 1997, there was an exhibition of popular cultural paraphrases of Munch's *The Scream* including kitsch. "Crossing the line from artwork to icon, a painting goes from being an object of contemplation to a form of public property," The *Toronto Star* (1 March 1997) wrote in its review of the exhibition. *The Scream* had become "a cash cow waiting to be milked." On the same occasion the art critic in the *Globe and Mail* (22 February 1997) maintained that "the strange usefulness of the picture has made it just about the most reproduced, parodied, caricatured, appropriated and downright popular high-art image in the world." Like the *Mona Lisa*, *Taj Mahal*, *Statue of Liberty*, and Marilyn Monroe, *The Scream* has become an icon "in almost the technical, sacred sense: the invisible made visible, the typical made specific . . . . With one difference. In the case of mass-culture icons, the invisible is not the Divine, but emotional experiences of ourselves and others, as sexy and victimized (Marilyn), or as inscrutable (the Mona Lisa), or as angst-ridden (The Scream)."

This transformation from work of art into icon has been made easier by the fact that postmodern culture to a much less extent than earlier eras distinguishes between high culture and popular culture. Here John Storey (1993: 16) notes two different reactions: "For some this is a reason to celebrate an end to an elitism constructed on arbitrary distinctions of culture, for others it is a reason to despair at the final victory of commerce over culture." The fact that the Munch Museum opposes what is regarded as the abuse of Munch's picture is in this connection natural and obvious. There is, of course, no getting away from the fact that the constant paraphrasing of *The Scream* in the long run threatens to influence our reading of the original picture in a direction contrary to Munch's pictorial idea. The flood of paraphrases and the wear that the paraphrases of popular culture lead to may gradually make it difficult to take Munch's work quite seriously. This in its turn may have repercussions for the kind of newspaper drawing that in a serious sense refers to *The Scream*, e.g., the drawings that have paraphrased the scream figure in connection with atomic bomb tests or with the terror act at Lockerbie. Unintentionally, these paraphrases refer at least as much to previous humorous paraphrases as to Munch's serious original. In consequence they lose in communicative power and become reduced to what John Hartley (1996: 45) says about *Iwo Jima*, the famous American photo from World War II: "It is just an image of itself, and refers only to our familiarity with it." In an article in *The Independent* Anna Somers Cocks wonders if *The Scream* has become "famous for being famous – rather than for the deeply meaningful experience we get from looking at her" (Cocks 1998). On the other hand it can equally be maintained that the paraphrase within popular culture has contributed to a broadening and consequently an enrichment of the experience that *The Scream* as a picture gives us. While other works of art at best lead a protected life in well-guarded museum buildings, for a long time *The Scream* functioned both on and beyond the museum wall, both within and outside the institution of art. The fact that *The Scream* has become one of the most important emblems of our time not only reveals much about the nature of our age; it also indicates a good deal about the power and quality of the picture itself.

Acknowledgments

Many thanks to Inger Engan, librarian at the Munch Museum, Oslo, for all her help, and to Ingrid Lund, who translated the text into English.

References

Aspenström, W. (2000). *Samlade dikter 1946–1997* (Collected Poems 1946–1997). Stockholm: Manpocket.

Bachtin, M. (1969). *Literatur und Karneval*. Munich: Carl Hauser Verlag.

Brookner, P. (1999). *A Concise Glossary of Cultural Theory*. London: Arnold.

Calinescu, M. (1997). Rewriting. In J. W. Bertens and D. Fokkema (eds.), *International Postmodernism: Theory and Literary Practice*. Amsterdam: John Benjamins.

Cocks, A. S. (1998). A Scream for our Times. *Independent*, 13 August. London.

Docker, J. (1994). *Postmodernism and Popular Culture: A Cultural History*. Cambridge: Cambridge University Press.

Dyer, R. (1977). *Gays and Film*. London: British Film Institute.

Fischer, J. (1984). Entitling. *Critical Enquiry* 11.

Genette, G. (1997). *Paratexts: Thresholds of Interpretation*. Jane E. Levin, trans. Cambridge: Cambridge University Press.

Haastrup, H. K. (1999). Scream – en intertextuell slasherfilm (Scream – an Intertextual Slasher Film). *Filmhäftet* 106. Stockholm.

Hall, S. (1997). *Representation: Cultural Representations and Signifying Practices*. London: Sage.

Hartley, J. (1966). *Popular Reality: Journalism, Modernity, Popular Culture*. London: Arnold.

Heller, R. (1973). *The Scream*. London: Viking Press.

Hoff, A. (1993). Skriket alle elsker (The Scream that Everybody Loves) *Arbeiderbladet*, 22 September. Oslo.

Levinson, J. (1985). Titles. *The Journal of Aesthetics and Art Criticism* 44: 2.

Lippman, W. (1993). Stereotypes. In *Public Opinion* (1922), reprinted in J. Corner and J. Hawthorn (eds.), *Communication Studies: An Introductory Reader* (4th ed.). London: Arnold.

Mays, J. B. (1997). Eeeeeeeeee!! *Globe and Mail*, 22 February.

Melly, G. (1977). Jokes about Modern Art. In G. Melly and J. R. Glaves-Smith (eds.), *A Child of Six Could Do It! Cartoons about Modern Art*. London: Tate.

Miller, J. H. (1992). *Illustration*. London: Reaktion Books.

Mirzoeff, N. (1999). *An Introduction to Visual Culture*. London and New York: Routledge.

Review of exhibit at the Art Gallery of Ontario in the *Toronto Star*, 1 March 1997 (reviewer unknown).

Storey, J. (1993). *Cultural Theory and Popular Culture* (2nd ed.). London and New York: Pearson.

Thompson, Della, ed. (1995). *The Concise Oxford Dictionary* (9th ed.). Oxford: Oxford
    University Press.
Walker, J. A. (1994). *Art in the Age of Mass Media*. London: Pluto Press.
Zaloscer, H. (1985). *Der Schrei. Signum einer Epoche*. Wien: Boehlau.

Filmography

Craven, W. (Director) (1996). *Scream*. US: Dimension Films.

THE HOLY LANCE AS LATE TWENTIETH-CENTURY SUBCULTURAL ICON

Volker Schier and Corine Schleif

The Holy Lance as Material Object Fixed in Space and Time

The Holy Lance (Figure 5.1) is displayed for public viewing in a glass case in the Treasury of the Vienna Hofburg. The objects immediately surrounding the lance are pieces from the imperial insignia of the Holy Roman Empire of the German Nation. This collection of signs that legitimated the emperor was amassed largely by Charles IV in the fourteenth century and included the crown and the scepter, Charlemagne's gloves and his priestly vestments, a splinter from the manger, a tooth of John the Baptist, and links from the chain used to fetter St. Peter. A cast lead pilgrim's badge from the fourteenth century survives in the city museum in Prague, and shows Charles displaying the lance to pilgrims who have come there for the annual display of the imperial insignia (Figure 5.2).

In 1424 the imperial insignia were brought to Nuremberg, where they were displayed in an elaborate civic spectacle liturgically known as the *Festum de Lancea et Armorum Christi*, literally the "Feast of the Lance and the Arms [or Weapons] of Christ." The annual event, referred to in

We thank Franz Kirchweger, Helmut Trnek, Jeffrey Vallance, Rosamund Felsen Gallery, and Lehmann Maupin Gallery for materials and information. This chapter draws on research for our forthcoming book on the Holy Lance. While this publication was in preparation we authored Die Heilige und die unheilige Lanze: Von Richard Wagner bis zum World Wide Web. In F. Kirchweger (ed.), *Die Heilige Lanze in Wien: Insignie – Reliquie – Schicksalsspeer*, 110–43. Vienna and Milan: Skira, 2005,

Figure 5.1 Holy Lance.
Kunsthistorisches Museum,
Vienna.

Figure 5.2 Pilgrim's Badge. Muzeum
hlavniho mesta Prahy, Prague.

the German vernacular as *Heiltum* (meaning simply "holy objects"), was accompanied by a fair that attracted buyers and sellers into the city by freeing them from certain taxes and tolls. A woodcut published by the city council in 1487 shows the imperial insignia being exhibited from a high platform on the market square. This ceremony took place once a year until the adoption of the Reformation in 1525.[1] Nonetheless, the imperial insignia were kept in Nuremberg until 1796, when they were first taken to Regensburg and subsequently, in 1800, to Vienna, where they have remained ever since with the exception of a brief return to Nuremberg during the Third Reich.

According to museum labeling, the lance bears the inventory number XIII 19; is Carolingian; dates from the eighth century; is made of steel, iron, brass, silver, gold, and leather; and is 50.7 centimeters long.[2] According to Helmut Trnek in the treasury's guide book, the tip of the blade of the lance was broken off at some unknown time – probably on one of the occasions when it was replicated. The two parts are now joined by a steel band and the damage and repairs are masked by two sheaths. The inner one of silver, dating from Henry IV in the eleventh century, is covered by a later one of gold. Both bear Latin inscriptions referring to the lance and the "nail of the Lord." A forged iron pin, from a distance resembling a spike or large nail, has been fitted lengthwise into an opening in the center of the tip and fastened by means of wire secured by knots. The pin has been embellished with tiny crosses visible between the knots in the wire. The crosses were first etched into the surface and then inlayed in brass. Two knife blades from the seventh and eighth centuries respectively have been affixed to the lance laterally by means of leather thongs, thus filling in the sections between the wings and the original blades. Thus the accidents and intentions of history are embedded in the object itself, which tells its own biography – or parts of it – to anyone informed enough to read the events from the material surfaces.

Unlike many other pieces in the imperial insignia displayed in the treasury, the lance cannot easily be considered a work of art. It is, rather, a hand weapon, albeit one that has been damaged, repaired, and altered in ways that prohibit its use as a weapon. It is likewise these changes that lend a distinctive appearance to the piece and define it as a specific one-of-a-kind object, thus assuring its recognition in various kinds of representations, ranging from simple line drawings to three-dimensional facsimile reproductions.

The lance is a material object, inanimate and small enough to be held in one's hands. With its clear-cut contours, distinctive surfaces, and small dimensions it willingly lends itself to appropriations, physical or conceptual. As we will observe, it has become a fetish, a historical object that contains the enduring material form of a singular event thus readily serving as the object of meaningful fixation (Apter and Pietz 1993: 3). As a simple utilitarian object, the lance itself makes no claims to represent something outside of itself, as does a monument, picture, or road sign. It is of itself, neither abstract – nor easily abstracted – nor does it call out to its viewers as a figure.

Nonetheless as an icon it has come to stand for a variety of other things. Likewise as an icon, its most basic meanings are communicated very directly through the appearance of the object. Charles Sanders Peirce used the term *icon* in his threefold categorization of signs. While the *index* is merely connected to what it signifies – physically or causally – and the *symbol* is assigned arbitrarily as a carrier of meaning, the *icon* is the least abstract and most transparent. This sign functions on the basis of identity or likeness. The signifier claims to be or to look like that which it signifies (Peirce 1993).

The icon, like a word, belongs to everyone who uses it. The Holy Lance, however, as a specific cultural icon with a specific individual identity, seems to exist somewhere between the realms of general signs like words and pictures, and that of specific objects that can be held in possession or that of words or pictures with proper names like trademarks. Unlike computer icons or trademarks, which are protected by copyright, the lance, although it can most certainly be taken into possession and can be – in fact it is – owned, cannot be used as a trademark because it is not a mark, that is, a kind of sign that has been invented.

It appears that almost from its beginnings, the lance was believed to be the one that pierced the side of Christ at the Crucifixion. Even earlier, as pious legends developed in the first centuries of Christianity, the name Longinus had been given to the captain who, according to John 19:34, thrust his spear into the side of Christ. The spear bearer, Longinus, was thus one of the standard elements of the first Crucifixion scenes.

The primary sign for the Crucifixion story, Christ, and Christianity came to be the cross. As Rainer Kahsnitz (1982) demonstrates, it was first necessary for the cross to be distanced from the grim yet banal realities of executions in order to become a positive and edifying Christian symbol. This had happened already by the fourth century when crucifixion was no longer used as a means of capital punishment. Valentin Groebner (1999) and Mitchell Merback (1998) have pointed to connections between late-medieval public executions and representations of the crucified Christ. Building on their observations regarding late-medieval culture, we might further observe that the cross could only then, once again, become a positive symbol for a large, many-faceted, and in no way unified or systematic set of beliefs, when these practices too were no longer so prevalent. Gold pendants worn as necklaces, crosses crowning steeple tops and marking the highest points of villages and towns nestling in European and American landscapes, and a simple character typed in front of the designation of a year denoting the end of the life of an individual – none of these modern phenomena serve as reminders of instruments of execution and torture. All are examples of inverse decoding in order to achieve meanings that are at variance to the original meanings of the cross (Tomaselli 1999: 38).

Similarly the lance became a positive Christian sign. However, unlike the cross, it was never completely separated from its initial use as a weapon. Spears or spear-like weapons continue to be produced and used. Even in subcultural re-presentations of the lance that attempt to abstract or aestheticize it, it never loses its deadly character. Its persistent definition as a weapon of hand-to-hand combat helped to perpetuate its recuperable meanings while also inviting new ones. In fact, some representations of the lance in action with a honed point and sharp edges make it appear far more deadly than the dull blunt object that rests in the glass case in Vienna.

Our search for the lance in the late twentieth century has taken us to nine novels, one computer game, one TV documentary, two TV series, one animated film, recorded music, comic books, web pages, and a performance artist. In fact, even as this article goes to press new material on the lance is being released. We have chosen to scrutinize the lance primarily as a *sub*cultural icon because it appears not to belong to any mainstream culture during this period. We will explore how the lance is claimed by groups with differing, yet sometimes related or overlapping agendas. Like the emperors who employed it to legitimate their claims to authority, late twentieth-century groups similarly used it to suggest certain kinds of exclusive access to power. Unlike the emperors, however, this legitimation enjoyed no universal recognition, but rather was/is limited to enclaves of "believers" and members of particular communities.

The Lance Unbound in Books

The story begins with *The Spear of Destiny*, first published by Trevor Ravenscroft in 1973. Written as nonfiction, replete with documentary photographs of historical figures, archival sources, and physical artifacts, Ravenscroft's book purports to demonstrate "the occult power behind the spear that pierced the side of Christ." Ravenscroft's real obsession, however, was the Faustian pact with evil into which many of the personalities that dominate our perception of history supposedly had entered, in order to achieve their final goal: world domination. Ravenscroft's list of forty-five emperors who had claimed the Spear of Destiny contains the expected protagonists – Constantine, Charlemagne, Napoleon, and, the main adversary, Hitler. Each leader had, at some point, chosen which of the two opposing "spirits" of the lance he would employ "in the fulfillment of his world historic aims" (Ravenscroft 1982: 22). Adolf Hitler was the historical figure who came closest to succeeding in using the dark powers of the lance to found an empire of evil. Hitler purportedly saw himself as the Carolingian Landulf II of Capua, whom Ravenscroft equates with the "true Klingsor," the villain in Richard Wagner's *Parcival*. Hitler felt compelled to possess the lance, and he was indeed possessed by it. It had been Hitler's "indelible conviction [that he] would one day step forward to claim the Spear of Destiny as his own personal possession and . . . he would fulfill a world-historic role with it" (Ravenscroft 1982: 21). Under the sway of this object, he became the supreme physical embodiment and superhuman perpetrator of evil.

Ravenscroft wove a clumsy pseudoscientific narrative, first by select-ing specific facts and data from press reports, such as the name of Julius Linke, the architect responsible for preserving many of Nuremberg's art treasures during World War II, or the name, rank and serial number of Walter Horn, the American officer who secured the imperial regalia upon the fall of Nuremberg (Ravenscroft 1982: 346). Ravenscroft then produced "false facts," for example, the assertion that Horn became a sociologist at the University of California, Berkeley. Indeed, Professor Horn was an art historian. Ravenscroft authenticated his tale by means of eyewitness accounts of Dr. Johannes Stein, who had hoped to write the book himself, but had died. Stein, purportedly a pupil of Rudolf Steiner, founder of the anthroposophical movement, claimed to have discovered Hitler's evil proclivities at an early stage in his rise to power. Ravenscroft contended that Stein had fled to England to become a personal advisor to Winston Churchill on matters of the occult and on the mind of Hitler. Ravenscroft (1982: xv) was able to meld unverifiable factual specifici-ties with quotations from Hitler and others, to which he alleges access through the use of occult faculties, the practice of mind expansion, and the gift of clairvoyance. A photograph or perhaps photomontage from 1938 shows Hitler standing in front of a glass case, viewing the imperial regalia. It was probably on the basis of this image that Ravenscroft spun a complex narrative, claiming that as a youth in Vienna in 1909, Hitler had had his first contact with the Holy Lance. Standing before the case, he could feel "something strange and powerful emanating from the iron spearhead, which he could not readily identify." Ravenscroft often lapses into the first person, as if Hitler were uttering the words: "I slowly became aware of a mighty presence around it – the same awesome presence which I had experienced inwardly on those rare occasions in my life when I had sensed that a great destiny awaited me . . . . A window in the future was opened up to me through which I saw in a single flash of illumination a future event by which I knew beyond contradiction that the blood in my veins would one day become the vessel of the Folk-Spirit of my people"

(Ravenscroft 1982: 20). Using the motif of reincarnation, Ravenscroft fashioned an ongoing series contouring the struggle between good and evil, or, as one online reviewer put it: in Ravencroft's book, "World War Two was really a conflict between famous ninth-century figures reincarnated after exactly one thousand years."[3]

In 1978, five years after the appearance of *The Spear of Destiny*, James Herbert (1999), author of chiller fiction such as *The Fog*, published his novel *The Spear*. Herbert contrives a horror story in which the forces of the lance revitalize the corpse of Heinrich Himmler. Nazis surviving the Third Reich team up with a group of British neo-Nazis to plot a terrorist attack. Herbert refers to the lance as "the weapon that pierced the side of Christ as he died on the cross." Similarly Herbert appropriates Ravenscroft's quotations from Wolfram von Eschenbach, Richard Wagner, Himmler, and Hitler – all of whom purportedly "witnessed" the power of the lance. For example, one of the fictional Nazis reports that "Hitler found the spearhead in Vienna's Hofburg Museum when he was little more than a vagrant in the city and made an extensive search into its history. Even at that time his head was filled with the past glories of the German people – and the glories yet to come. He also had visions of other battles, those fought in other dimensions, mystical wars between the forces of God and the forces of the Devil" (1999: 150). In 1979 a British court ruled that Herbert had plagiarized Ravenscroft, using this work of "nonfiction" to give his novel a "backcloth of apparent truth." After summarizing Herbert's story the judge commented, "One must not underestimate the commercial attraction of the rubbish I have attempted to describe" (Anderson 1995: 89–90). Ironically, however, it may have been vivid accounts of violence wrought by super weapons and mysterious events like those related by Herbert that actually authenticated Ravenscroft's "historical facts," at least within that segment of society that purchased this literature. Indeed the genres of fiction and nonfiction appear to meld as the preoccupation with the paranormal, unlike the case of the precursor genre of science fiction, seeks to establish its authenticity not on the futuristic promises of science but from the eyewitness evidence of historical documentation. Ravenscroft's book, a modest success when originally published in the US, came to acquire widespread acclaim in the early 1990s after other related books had appeared and associated material became available on the Internet. The book has been translated into seventeen languages and undergone numerous printings in English.

Howard Buechner, who claims to be an American physician and to have participated in the liberation of the concentration camp at Dachau, and Wilhelm Bernhart, who alleges to have been a German naval officer during World War II and writing under a pseudonym, collaborated to publish *Adolf Hitler and the Secrets of the Holy Lance*. The book acknowledges contributions of numerous individuals, some with doctor or professor titles, some with institutional affiliations, some with special areas of expertise in the US and Germany – although a close look at the list may elicit a chuckle from anyone who notices that a woman who carried out pictorial research is identified as "Mrs. Helen Huppertz, Am Bahnhof [at the train station], West Germany" (Buechner and Bernhard 1989: 12). The narrative takes up where Ravenscroft's story left off. Employing abundant detail including evidence in the form of documents, photographs, and diagrams, the authors spin an account of how the lance was "rescued" just before the Allies took Berlin. Bernhart asserts he was aboard the U 530, one of the two specially outfitted submarines that the Nazis commissioned to take the lance to "Neu Schwabenland" in Antarctica, where it was placed in a hidden cave in the ice. In Europe, a Japanese master sword maker is said to have forged a replica – the object now on view in the Hofburg in Vienna. Buechner and Bernhart published a sequel a year later, *Hitler's Ashes – Seeds of a New Reich*, in which they discuss the exploits of the Order of the Knights of the Holy Lance, whose task it has been since 1979 to retrieve the lance and to guard it at an undisclosed location in Germany. Generally, Ravenscroft had admired and feared the occult power of Hitler's lance; in contrast, Buechner and Bernhart esteem it, envy it, and wish to perpetuate it.

In 1990, in an endeavor to capitalize further on the success of the *Spear of Destiny*, Ravenscroft together with Tim Wallace-Murphy published *The Mark of the Beast: The Continuing Story of the Spear of Destiny*. With missionary zeal the authors make a direct appeal to their audience: "The purpose of this second volume is to enable you the reader to use the powers of the Spear to gain a new and deeper insight into the unfolding pattern of your own life" (Ravenscroft and Wallace-Murphy 1990: 3). They write of the apocalyptic character of their task: "Using these faculties associated with the Spear of Destiny we will interpret the strange mythological symbolism of the Revelation of St. John in everyday, rational and scientific terms. And in such a manner describe the nature of the coming global catastrophes at the commencement of the epoch which will culminate in the appearance of the Great Dictator and Anti Christ" (1990: 3). The authors make the lance – or Hitler's possession of it – responsible for the worst atrocities of the Third Reich. Again, historical specificities are conjured up. For example, it is asserted that evidence was provided at the Nuremberg international war crimes tribunal that the very night Hitler gained access to the lance he had decided to enact the "Final Solution" and annihilate non-Aryans (1990: 9). Here too, ironically, the text is colored by nationalism. The authors delineate a "folk soul" both in Germany and in Britain (1990: 25–26). In the latter case, it was Alfred the Great who formed this spirit, a spirit that departed with the death of Churchill whose final task it had been to conquer Nazi Germany.

In 1992 Bill Still published *Legend of the Holy Lance, A Novel*. In his preface he states, "The Holy Lance of Longinus is real. The historical basis upon which this work of fiction rests is as accurate as any tale based upon ancient legends can be" (Still 1992: vii). Still draws his "facts" from the aforementioned books, especially Buechner and Bernhart, without citing them directly. For example, after writing that the lance had been retrieved from Antarctica, Still asserts that only Rudolf Hess, incarcerated in Berlin, where he served a life sentence for Nazi war crimes, was aware of its location. Still attempts to persuade his readers that the entire world is controlled by two rival secret societies: the Black Knights, who overtly venerate evil, and the White Knights, who feign the pursuit of goodness to disguise their attempts at world domination. The author tries to convince readers that the dangers of these secret societies likewise abound in high places within the US. The American wing of the Black Knights is the Skull and Bones Society, centered at Yale University. A freelance reporter, Jim Windsor, investigates this society for the Washington Post because an American vice-president with a Yale degree and member of this confraternity – thinly disguised with the name Harriman Schiff but clearly resembling George H. W. Bush – is said to be in line for his party's presidential nomination. Both societies are dominated by German nationalists, striving for German reunification. The two vie for possession of the lance in order to avail themselves of its power.

According to Still, not just anyone can touch the lance – only a true Merovingian can. Merovingians trace their lineage back to the carnal union of Jesus Christ and Mary Magdalene, an illicit relationship, according to Still, that cost Christ his divinity and brought about his demotion to prophet status. Hitler burnt his hands when he tried to touch the lance; Himmler, however, as a true Merovingian, was able to hold it. The *Spear of Destiny* had extended the legendary biography of this weapon beyond the Middle Ages and incorporated the Hitler legends. Still places the roots of the spear before its use by Longinus at the time of the Crucifixion: he writes that it was forged in 3062 BC by the ancient metalsmith Tubal-Cain, and that it was made from a meteorite, at that time the only source of iron.

More religious in tone is Clint Kelly's *The Aryan* (1995), in which neo-Nazi terrorists steal all the major relics of the Roman Catholic Church in order to force governments to allow them to assume world domination. It is from the lance that they hope to draw power and achieve legitimation. Like other authors, Kelly borrows elements and characters from previous works, sometimes with little attention to accuracy. For example, it is William (not Walter) Horn who seizes the lance for the Allies

at the close of World War II. In the end, the terrorists capitulate, after being convinced, falsely, that the lance in their possession is not the Holy Lance.

A novel that usurps many elements from the earlier books is Richard Greenwald's (1996) *The Spear of Golgotha*, a James Bond-like adventure story that combines sultry sex, miraculous healing, speeding Harleys, bioelectric fields, aging Nazis, and glowing crosses. Another, *The Spear of Tyranny: A Prophetic Novel* by Grant Jeffrey and Angela Hunt (2000), involves a conspiracy for world domination depending on the possession of the lance. Here, the grand narrative is drawn into the future. The evil Adrian Romulus is chosen world leader after a devastating global war that produces a longing for a stable new world order. He achieves total hegemony over the entire population, with the exception of a group of Jews who refuse to allow microchips to be implanted, a measure imposed in an effort to identify and control every living person. In their resistance they begin to accept biblical (Christian) prophecy.

In 1995, journalist Ken Anderson approached the Holy Lance from a different angle. His *Hitler and the Occult* debunks notions of Hitler's connections with the occult, particularly the associations with the lance as put forth by Ravenscroft. Although Anderson disputes Ravenscroft, his work rides in the wake of the *Spear of Destiny* and similar books in that he takes the works seriously enough to embark on a crusade to set their "facts" straight. In addressing this topic he likewise capitalizes on their sensationalism.

The covers of these books sport the red, black, and gold of the German flag. Buechner and Bernhart's bears the red, black, and white of Hitler's Third Reich, along with the associated swastika on which is superimposed a photograph of the now sharpened tip of the lance, unwrapped to expose its constituent parts – blade, pin, and wire. With the exception of Anderson and Kelly's *The Aryan*, all include a picture of the lance. Herbert's horror story shows a long slender spear glowing from a distance. All the others include a representation of the lance with the articulation of enough details to ensure association with the lance displayed in the glass case in Vienna. The cover illustration of *The Mark of the Beast* (Figure 5.3) telescopes the history of the Holy Lance into one picture by projecting a close-up vertical image of the lance against a background that combines a seascape showing a cavernous icy bay and four skeletal horsemen approaching out of the sky – suggesting the Four Horsemen of the Apocalypse, all of whom together with their horses are clad in armor. The most striking cover design is that of *The Spear of Tyranny* (Figure 5.4), which is dominated by the piercing stare of two large eyes, peering out from behind a small blurred image of the Temple in Jerusalem, and framed at the bottom by a pixilated image of the lance.

Figure 5.3 Cover of Trevor Ravenscroft and Tim Wallace-Murphy, *The Mark of the Beast: The Continuing Story of the Spear of Destiny.*

Figure 5.4 Cover of Grant R. Jeffrey and Angela Hunt, *The Spear of Tyranny*.

Together these texts and images draw on the titillating effects of potential violence, the allure of the supernatural or the occult, the fascination with the terrors of the Third Reich, and the attraction of what might be called a (photo-) journalistic approach to history – including biblical history. The books engender communities of readers, an aim that may supersede that of monetary gain from their sales.

The Lance Drawn into Comics

Another traditional medium that employed the lance as both an object and a protagonist in a wide range of adventure stories is the comic book. In the *Last Days of the Justice Society of America*, published by DC Comics in 1986, the lance was again used to focus attention on World War II. Drawing on Ravenscroft and others, the comic writers suggest that it is the lance that makes dictators like Hitler and Mussolini invincible against characters such as Superman and the Spector. After Hitler destroys the world using the lance, the Justice Society sets out to bring the world back, all of which occurs in a parallel world of Germanic gods and magic.

A series of *Indiana Jones* comics published by Dark Horse Comics (1995) continues the narrative from the film *Indiana Jones and the Last Crusade* that focused on archeologist Indiana Jones and his literary historian father in their (successful) quest to retrieve the Holy Grail (Lee, Simpson, and Spiegle 1995). Much of the adventure involves reuniting the lance with its staff. Here, as in other narratives, the presence and integrity of the lance in Vienna must in some way be denied or questioned to make the object more elusive and enable the protagonists to vie for possession of the one true lance. Here, it has been rendered incomplete. The last frame shows the lance floating in front of a mushroom cloud (Figure 5.5). Over the cloud are the words: "It is said that he who claims the spear and solves its mystery holds the fate of the world in his hands . . . for good or for evil!" Here, the fear and awe of nuclear power and its potential for good and evil are unambiguously articulated. Not only are memories of World War II recalled but also the alarm and hopeful dreams associated with nuclear energy in the 1950s.

The Darkness: Spear of Destiny, published by Top Cow Productions in 2000, features "The Magdalena," an agent of the Vatican for special missions. This story is composed primarily of grandiose and exacting pictures accompanied by sparsely suggestive dialogue peppered with understated quips, gasps, sighs, and other noises. Historic flashbacks specify how every generation has its own Magdalena, who is always a direct descendant of the biblical Mary Magdalene; one of them had forced the Spear of Destiny from the hands of Hitler at the end of the war (Figure 5.6). Through rituals evocative of Christian rites of baptism and the Eucharist, each Magdalena is inducted into her office and endowed with the secret power

Figure 5.5 Illustration from: Elaine Lee, Will Simpson, and Dan Spiegle, *Indiana Jones and the Spear of Destiny*, vol. 4.

of light that enables her to do battle against evil. Although the hero of the narrative was issued the Holy Lance (sometimes referred to in the dialogue as "the sepulcher") by the Vatican, the performance of the initiation rite was omitted, rendering Magdalena vulnerable. Consequently, she loses the lance and encounters grave difficulties when she is dispatched to kill the personification of evil, Jackie Estacado, a New York mobster, who can morph into a hybrid creature reminiscent of the figure of the classic horror film *The Fly*, with humanoid and insect-like parts or a writhing, many-headed serpent-like monster more terrible than that which killed Laocoon. Because Magdalena is belatedly bestowed with supernatural powers, she is doomed to martyrdom by crucifixion. The final image shows her clad in only a G-string, head bowed, limbs pinned with daggers to the wood of a cross (Figure 5.7).

Figure 5.6 Illustration from Benitez et al., *Spear of Destiny*. Series: The Darkness 15–18.

Figure 5.7 Illustration from Benitez et al. *Spear of Destiny*. Series: The Darkness 15–18.

Like "lawful combatants" sporting their national emblems on their uniforms, Magdalena wears the cross. Like a medieval crusader she fights for the cross and like Joan of Arc she dies in this struggle, although her realization of Christian theology is based not on forgiveness, but on the eradication of a personified and demonized evil that even takes on hybrid forms not unlike the enigmatic depictions once scorned by Saint Bernard in the twelfth century – a concept and a visualization long abandoned by the Catholic Church. The Holy Lance is the most potent weapon against evil. As in the Middle Ages, it once again belongs to the *arma Christi*, although here not in keeping with its medieval significance as an instrument of salvation. As seen, many narratives – even those of Indiana Jones – employ the lance to fashion violent masculinities. However, "The Magdalena" is based on gender reversals in which an androgynous female character succeeds in possessing the phallus and thereby serves both to underscore and to challenge dominant gender constructions.

The comic appropriates the lance to portray violence in its simplest and perhaps most archetypal form. Pointed and sharp, it can be easily wielded and thrust to pierce the body of an opponent. True to the medium, the comic book lance – especially that of Magdalena – serves both to glorify violence and to render it harmless. Aesthetisized through dramatic views and poses, cinematographically designed stills and sequences, striking color combinations, as well as slick surfaces, all delineated by the ever-present black lines most characteristic of comics, these pictures distance the viewer, rather than facilitate empathy for physical or emotional pain. Even the blood from the severed bodies of monsters does not spill out beyond the confining boundaries of the black outlines. Thus violence remains tamed and controlled within the borders of that perfect world defined by the style of the Disney cartoon. The violent figure of Magdalena incorporates not only the heroic qualities of the saintly Joan of Arc with the transgressive appearance of Madonna, but also with the orderly and benign characteristics of Snow White. The black lines, not unlike the boundaries of children's coloring books that restrict and regulate, are here completely obeyed. Nothing can escape the controls of the black lines on the pages and prove harmful to the viewer-reader.

The Lance Darting through Cyberspace

Like the older medium, words and pictures printed on paper, the Internet encompasses countless literary and pictorial genres. Further, it permits nearly uncontrolled dissemination combined with unlimited capabilities for multidirectional communication. Boundaries between producers and recipients, authors and audiences are thus blurred. Individuals and groups can dispatch, receive, and exchange material with or without finding and joining each other. All this is accomplished without the regulating factors that market forces usually impose. The internet is anarchic in that no ordering principles from the Library of Congress or other reader, researcher, or author-initiated systems are in force to channel and control knowledge. Nonetheless, new ordering principles and connecting tools have emerged to facilitate access to and retrieval of endless streams of data. In 2000 Google identified 75,000 documents that mentioned "holy" and "lance." Of course, not all of these pertained to *the* Holy Lance.

In some respects the new medium is impatient, fickle, and mercurial, in that its information can be altered and even disappear at the press of a button, or its organizational hierarchies can be rearranged without notice or apparent reason. In February 2002, the first search result for "holy lance" registered by Google was not the Holy Lance displayed in the Vienna Hofburg, but that in the Museum of Unnatural Mystery.[4] The "curator," Lee Krystek, describes his collection as a "slightly bizarre cyberspace science museum for all ages" that – in addition to the Holy Lance – contains attractions such as the "Hall of UFO mysteries," the "Lost World Exhibition," and a "Dinosaur Safari." The metaphor of the museum extends to another feature of the site, the cybermuseum gift shop, which perhaps alludes to the profit motive that may have induced the owner to negotiate his placement as the first item in the list of search results.

In January 2002, the item at the top of the list for Google was an entry on the Holy Lance from the Catholic Encyclopedia.[5] Upon further examination it became clear that the article was drawn from the 1910 edition, which is no longer copyrighted. Perusing the available links at the site, one realizes that the page is subsidized by advertisers who target Catholic users in their marketing of certain religious goods or services: for example, books and gifts specifically for Catholics, offers of tours to various shrines and pilgrimage sites, or "Ave Maria Single Catholics" – a dating service. Thus both of these sites indirectly commodify the lance, one in the Sci-Fi context, the other within Roman Catholic venues.

During 2001 the website *The Lance, the Swastika, and the Merovingians* belonging to William Kalogonis headed the list.[6] Here, an introductory page sports a swastika, a fleur-de-lis, and the lance superimposed over each other. It is dedicated to "publicizing the links between Nazism and the occult as well as other possible links between the occult and other modern political organizations." The theme of this brief two-page summary of "facts" is the continuing quest for possession of the lance and its passage through history as it changed hands from one world leader to the next. Kalogonis warns of the power of the lance and specific details are incorporated to lend an air of scientific or historical credence. Similarly, the name and serial number of Walter Horn are again part of the narrative.

Hyperlinks that serve as markers leading the user from one web page to another constitute an important device that structures and orders knowledge on the Internet. This process of linking creates a text that is stabilized, expanded, modified, and/or distorted by every new web page accessed. The procedure likewise entices users to add their own information, to reconnect existing material through new hyperlinks, and to glimpse those phantoms of web pages that are no longer in place but faintly echoed by missing links.

These mechanisms facilitate the spinning out of the already-reported published tales of the lance in Antarctica and two rival secret societies into ever-widening conspiracy theories. At its site, the International Society for a Complete Earth explains that the group was founded by the anonymous Captain Ritter von X, who alleges to have been present on the submarine that brought the lance to Antarctica.[7] If this delirious tale sounds familiar, it is because its author is credited as the coauthor of the aforementioned books *Adolf Hitler and the Secrets of the Holy Lance* and *Hitler's Ashes*. The society, whose emblem is a swastika, aims to enter one of the polar openings and contact the Arianni, a "tall blond, blue-eyed super-race that rules the inner world." The Arianni speak a language very much like German, live in cities built of shimmering crystal, and use a kind of flying saucer called a *flugelrod* "to patrol the skies of the surface world and keep an eye on us."

Another site, headlined *Study Antichrist through Study of Hitler*, is owned by Cutting Edge Ministries, who support "fundamental Bible-believing churches."[8] Believing in the occult properties of the lance and perceiving it as an extension of biblical prophecy, the authors go to great lengths to paint word pictures of Hitler's terror interspersed with apocalyptic warnings from the Old and New Testaments. Citing Ravenscroft's assertion that the "Beast does not look like what he is," they go on to write that this description "can also be applied to most men today who are working mightily to stage the coming Antichrist, George Bush, Gerald Ford, Jimmy Carter, all looked so normal; yet, they worked very hard to effect the changes necessary to bring about the New World Order." The treatise ends by asking visitors: "Are you spiritually ready? Is your family? Are you adequately protecting your loved ones?" This is followed by a directive to be "born again."

All of the above play on fears of worldwide conspiracies, of worldwide peacekeeping institutions, of governments, of governmental agencies including social agencies and those promoting multiculturalism, as well as above all the New World Order (NWO). Fundamentalist religious groups appropriate the Holy Lance with its numinous properties as a vehicle to extend the purview of the miraculous out of and beyond the biblical context and provide supernatural interventions in contemporary life, to which they are privy by way of their exclusive knowledge of biblical prophesy and their transhistorical identification with "the righteous." It is this elitist knowledge that they commodify and offer for purchase to whomever will join their ranks by committing themselves and their resources of time and money. Neo-Nazi groups likewise proselytize using the lance and seek support in the form of subscriptions and donations, creating demand by rarefying and mystifying their fascist and racist pursuits sometimes under the cover of the secrecy permitted through the disembodied identities of the Internet (Zickmund 1997).

For such nongeographic communities, cyberspace offers places of sanctuary and exchange that replace churches, temples, coffee shops, bars, and meeting houses. Members of cybercommunities inhabit these worlds and live out realities that are possible only where the camouflaging elements in which they were cloaked by "conspiracist-controlled" mainstream culture appear removed, allowing an unhindered access to and retrieval of the "truth out there." The lance assumes significance for these subcultures because it signals violence, power, and danger at the most basic level using the most iconic means. Equally important, it connects a subculture to purported mainstream roots in the culture(s) of the past, thus enabling a subculture to make a claim to ultimate and universal legitimacy although marginalized in the world of the present. Here, the cyber possibilities of mixing and melding past, present, and future play a momentous role.[9]

Paradoxically, all of these groups suspend the lance in a belief system supported on the one hand by verifiable, natural, and historical "facts," and on the other hand by faith in the occult, paranormal, and supernatural. One "dot com" that carries several publications featuring the Holy Lance and markets items on a variety of topics ranging from ancient mysteries to lost worlds, mystic travel, antigravity, and right-wing propaganda includes the following satirical disclaimer on its website: "Warning! The contents of the Adventures Unlimited catalog can be hazardous to your belief system. The books and videos contained within have been known to cause stress to pat answers, simple explanations, and on occasion, to change opinions entirely." Belief in the observable yet inexplicable is at the heart of the mythology of the lance. Many paths for the transference of power from one leader to the next have enjoyed cultural legitimacy. Some channels are hereditary and can be described variously as dynastic or genetic, and are usually patriarchal. In other cases, power is shared and circulated among office holders who rule by some form of consensus and for the good of the commonweal. The perception of the Holy Lance as the vehicle for the transference of power from one world leader to the next rests on a belief in the constant and direct intervention of supernatural forces, either residing in the Lance itself, or operating on it from the outside.

The Holy Lance exists within the textual fabric John Fiske (1989: 103–04) describes as "producerly" in that it is open for and based on rereading and rewriting. Nonetheless, through this process, a broad but relatively stable overarching and polyvocal metatext has congealed around the Lance, that contains characteristic elements accepted by a wide spectrum of subcultures. The creation of this metatext is based on the ongoing reception, emulation, interpretation, and adaptation of the many linked and unlinked texts. These mechanisms also facilitate the necessary filling in of the missing parts within the narrative. This metatext is subsequently woven into larger, often opposing textual structures and appropriated by a wide array of groups with often differing aims. At this level we see the group-specific interpretation of the elements encoded in the metatext in ways that do not pretend to bridge the wide ideological gaps between the groups employing it. For example, for many users the source of the "information" about the Holy Lance in Antarctica or knowledge of its authorship is unimportant. This knowledge has become an integral part of the metatext attached to the icon and is used by Christian fundamentalist, New Age, and neo-Nazi groups alike for the creation of their individual "worlds" and spaces to which they can escape. Thus, with the aid of the Internet, we perceive the emergence of a fact-based, diachronic history of the Holy Lance from antiquity to the present, that incorporates – among other elements – notions of binary forces of good and evil, "great men," and a nostalgia for a totalitarian past. The Lance has become the icon for verifiable (arti)factual history, for a panhistorical mythic past, for unexplainable powers and forces, and for the struggle of heroic warriors that continues into the present and the future.

Before leaving cyberspace, we wish to glance briefly at the genre of fan fiction. Here the ongoing (re)writing is conscious and transparent and can take the form of short stories and novellas or extensive "netbook" projects in which developers provide rough sketches of personalities and/or objects and solicit members of cyber-communities to create and develop the complex virtual worlds of computer games as a group effort. Kevin Webb's description of the "Spear of Destiny – A Relic for the Gothic Earth" for his netbook bearing the title *Book of Souls* and intended to provide a guide to the *Ravenloft* and *Gothic Earth* "campaign settings" expanding the computer game *Dungeons and Dragons* is very precise, reiterating many elements of the metatext. He not only specifies what material it is made of, oak and iron, but also states an exact length of twelve feet and weight of eight pounds, in addition to describing the lance's mythical power. He further provides curses that can be employed by its owner and even suggests methods for its destruction.[10] In the story *Lara Croft and the Spear of Destiny*, Sarah Crisman places the lance in the hands of the animated superhero of computer game and film fame – Lara Croft.[11] The resultant reading/writing of the metatext positions this female character in the line of great men who have possessed this phallic object. The incident, together with that of the comic book figure Magdalena, suggests that, although secret missions to Antarctica and flying saucers became plausible elements within the metatext of subcultural history writing, a woman protagonist was apparently only permissible in a genre that not only was flagrantly fiction, but also only acceptable for a woman that was disembodied either as the two-dimensional comic book figure Magdalena or the doll-like three-dimensional computer animation Lara Croft.[12]

The Holy Lance in Computer Games

The Holy Lance is also manifest in the computer game the *Spear of Destiny*, released by ID Software in 1992 (Figure 5.8). The task is to obtain the lance and to remain alive. This is accomplished by killing Nazi opponents represented primarily as uniformed World War II soldiers and SS troops. When the game first appeared it aroused considerable controversy, particularly in Germany. The original shock value involving uniformed Nazis was supplanted by a sequel in which the player can assume the identity of a Nazi protagonist. *Spear of Destiny* was a sophisticated and popular "first-person shooter," often emulated by the makers of subsequent computer games. The player can choose weapons and aim them as they appear at the lower edge of the screen. Traversing various rooms leading into other rooms, the player can acquire treasures as they appear, most of which vaguely resemble items among the imperial insignia in Vienna. Intent on maneuvering one's way through various passages in the quest for the lance, one must kill the guards along the way. When they are hit, splatters of blood appear; when they fall they cry out in pain or utter the words "Mein Leben!" (My life!). All this takes place to the accompaniment of music of the sort used as soundtrack for children's animated films, which trivializes the undertaking. Additional noises are of importance for the first person shooter's survival, for example, the sound of opening doors outside the scope of vision that are meant to deter or distract the player.

Why has the quest for the lance been rendered in this manner as a computer game? Certainly the game manifests more than a simple commercialized trivialization for the sake of entertainment. Indeed violence is here commodified – it was in fact possible to pay a fee and buy clues to the game that provide combinations of keys enabling the player to win by making him (or her) invincible, and thus superhuman. The player thus can hurt and kill the others, without having to fear virtual death. Further, this violence is justified in that it is the bad guys who are killed – indeed, the Nazis, history's worst. By annihilating Nazis the player is not merely

Figure 5.8 Illustration on box cover of computer game *Spear of Destiny* by ID Software.

doing a favor for humanity – after all, World War II had already been won by the Allies fifty years before. Rather, as in the fascination witnessed in other media, the player can feel exhilarated by conquering such a powerful and indeed (at least in terms of might) an admired foe. The successful player can claim the lance as a trophy. This weapon as trophy may be regarded as a fetish both in the Freudian sense, in other words as an ersatz object for the lost phallus, but also as a fetish in the more general anthropological sense, as a material object that is potent and valued. Thus, the two goals of the game, acquiring the lance and outliving the opponents on the screen, are conceptually linked since prowess can be obtained only through the lance.

The Holy Lance Reverberates through Sound Recordings

The Holy Lance has not only become a household name in traditional printed matter and electronic media, but also has found its way into popular music. It is interesting to note that in this medium the broadest spectrum of meanings has attached itself to this icon. The British rock group *Spear of Destiny* was formed following the dissolution of *The Pack* and *Theatre of Hate*, the latter famous for violent live acts in the early 1980s. With *Spear of Destiny*, the composer and songwriter Kirk Brandon achieved a more polished and marketable sound that brought the group live performances on BBC radio. The songs contain no direct reference to the Holy Lance. Even the additional notes the group provides in the liner of the CDs and on their web page do not offer an auctorial reading of the group's name. Thus listeners are challenged with the task of connecting the name to the lyrics and the music. The overarching theme in the 1997 album *Religion* is a state of society described as bleak, inhospitable, and deprived of all humanitarianism, which stands in antithesis to the world view of many proponents of the new electronic media, who optimistically pursue the promised social rewards of advanced technologies. Pessimistic lyrics tell of searches for meaning and purpose that cannot be found.

In the song "Prison Planet," Brandon addresses the loss of all spiritual guidance that now robs humankind of the possibility of fleeing the prison it has erected for itself by substituting objects – "insane machines" – for spiritual experience. Destiny, obviously the synonym for this prison, remains the only controlling factor of life, inescapable in its all-determining grasp. That Brandon is wary of some of the influence that modern technology exerts on society becomes fully evident in the final track, "Total Kontrol." The refrain, "total kontrol, nothing else will do," refers to the kind of totalitarian society pictured in the novel *1984* by George Orwell. The spelling informs us which side of the political spectrum he fears most: right-wing neo-Nazi groups, who in fact often distort or "Germanize" the spelling of English words. Especially telling is the lyric's description of the barcoding of people on the wrist, a reference to the tattooing of registration numbers on the arm of inmates in concentration camps.

Based in Brisbane, the group calling itself *Spear of Longinus* stands in marked contrast to *Spear of Destiny*. The group describes its music as "Nazi occult metal." Interviews with members of the group, who use pseudonyms, have been published on the official web page. The drummer and guitarist, Griffiths, is the most outspoken of the four. When asked by the anonymous interviewer where the band had got its name he replied: "Camazotz [another member of the group] was reading a book called *The Spear of Destiny* by Trevor Ravenscroft and he came up with the name *Spear of Longinus*. I like it because this is what ended the Xtian dog's life, very anti-Christ." According to Camazotz, the spear stands for the "phallus" and "alchemic aspect" that serve for "transmuting the sexual energies to create the solar man." The web page includes discussions of, and a link to another site calling for the release of the "black metal musician" Hendrik Möbus, an alleged perpetrator of hate crimes convicted and sentenced for murder.

Griffiths expresses his longing for a return to a mythic, mystic past and to a "simpler life" with "little or no major problems." Unlike *Spear of Destiny*, which does not offer solutions for the state of society in its songs, *Spear of Longinus* employs a naive analysis and proposes even more simplistic solutions. One of the main problems for Griffiths is the loss of identity due to the mixing of races. Political solutions can only be achieved through a strong-minded leader who rules with an iron fist. Change can only be wrought by force. For Camazotz, National Socialism embodies "all that is mighty, noble, just, imperishable and . . . archaik [*sic*], a true revival of the old ways." Griffiths wants the readers to know that his "beliefs" are extreme and that he himself is an "anti-Christ Nationalist." A crude mixture of Germanic Odinist mythology, occultism, Eastern philosophy, and even Satanism appears to provide the ideological underpinnings of the group. The lance functions as the icon for this belief system, since it is itself an ancient symbol that signifies not only power, but the direct exercise of power as unsullied, unblended violence. In the archaic world model promoted here, power is the only legitimating factor and violence its sole vehicle. The strong will inevitably rule the weak.

We observe that the evil powers Ravenscroft ascribes to the lance and narratizes as dangerous are taken up as positive by the members of *Spear of Longinus*. In this respect *Spear of Longinus* has subscribed to the metatext of the lance that evolved through books and Internet pages. Here, however, through a slight revision of the central kernel of the narrative, the story has been fundamentally rewritten: rather than perceiving the power of the lance as derived from its function as one of the instruments of Christ's passion and martyrdom, here it is glorified most drastically as the weapon that violently inflicted a wound in Christ and thus opposed Christianity. Thus, once again inverting the already inverted sign of the lance, the group brought its meaning full circle.

We have witnessed great differences in the messages, means, and aims of the music focusing on or employing the Holy Lance. Each of the examples addresses a distinct segment of society – a particular subcultural group. The music, like many of the literary and visual forms discussed so far, serves to hail individuals and to exhort them to seek identities as partisans belonging to variously defined groups. In all examples, whether from literature, music, the visual arts, or multimedia sources, membership in a particular group was restricted – in some important cases through race, ethnicity, or perhaps gender – but also often through the voluntary adherence to certain beliefs or belief systems.

Cult of Subcultures to the Mainstream of the Arts and Education Network

A documentary on the Holy Lance was broadcast in the US on the Arts and Education Network in 1995 and released as a video in 1996.[13] As a program in the series *Ancient Mysteries: New Investigations of the Unsolved*, the film *The Quest for the Holy Lance* traces the history of the lance from the time of Christ to the present day. The authors capitalize on a fascination with the supernatural by co-opting the sensationalism found in books like those by Ravenscroft and on the websites described above in order to tap it for marketing purposes. The sleeve touts the video as "compelling and awesome"; assuring that it will "provoke wonder." Further, it is promised that "facts and fables" will be uncovered and the question whether or not the story of the lance is really true will be addressed.

The film's reliability appears enhanced since it is a technically polished, high-budget production, and the "witnesses" of the specifics are endowed with mainstream credibility – be they recognizable works of art and architecture or recognized university professors. Nonetheless, the documentary often not only adopts global statements but appropriates the would-be supporting "facts" from the books and websites treated above. In fact even Howard and Emajean Buechner appear in the credits at the end of the film. Thus the inaccuracy of the historical facts is often shocking. For example, it is reported that Charlemagne held the lance while trying to capture Jerusalem – something he certainly never attempted. It is also stated that the lance was brought to Nuremberg in 1250 by Emperor Friedrich II and that it remained there for 550 years. Indeed, it was first given to the imperial city of Nuremberg by Emperor Sigismund in 1424.

Fact is also sacrificed to facticity in the juxtaposition of objects or images with verbal narration. For example, while viewers are instructed about the physical details of ancient Roman spears, they are shown the medieval copy of the Holy Lance in Krakow. Or, when Emperor Otto I is mentioned, viewers see a manuscript image of Otto III. Similarly the music provides juxtaposition in yet another dimension, although this juxtaposition is less blatantly deceptive. Accompanying the entire fifty minutes of the program with music, the makers draw from a limited repertoire of pieces, composed either for the program or the series to cause the images and the spoken text to resonate in a specific way: Music built on diatonic motifs and performed on plucked instruments is meant to create the ambience of antiquity, fanfares in the style of classic Hollywood movies suggest knightly heroism in the Middle Ages, and a neo-Romantic melody expresses the power of the lance. Interestingly, this musical ambience connoting the romantic hero not only backgrounds the nineteenth- and twentieth-century portions of the narrative, but much of the story of the lance in the Middle Ages as well. Similarly, many paintings and sculptures from the Renaissance are used to illustrate the biblical account of the lance from the first centuries.

The film closes by asserting that it matters not what really happened to the real Holy Lance: "What matters is what people believe – believe tracing back to a mystery that began two thousand years ago on a desolate hillside outside Jerusalem at the execution of a carpenter from Nazareth named Jesus." Taken at face value this sentence can be accepted by nearly anyone: belief colors perception and makes things happen. The last sentence of the film would certainly ring true to most Christians because it is devoid of any doctrine regarding the person or role of Jesus or any theology specifying the purpose or meaning of the Crucifixion – those issues that separate various denominations from each other. Uttered in reverent tones, these final words play to mainstream American religious sentiments that are belief based, yet just as much full of longing for evidence of the supernatural as they are desirous of stable transcendent meanings. Although the metanarrative of the various subcultural conspiracy theorists has been adopted, it has also been adapted and aestheticized to match the tastes of those who consider themselves middle-class, democratic, law abiding citizens.

The Lance Veiled and Unveiled by the Performance/ Conceptual Artist Jeffrey Vallance

After having scrutinized the Holy Lance in the Hofburg in Vienna and studied its history, American artist Jeffrey Vallance forged a copy of the lance under the guidance and direction of a metalsmith (Figure 5.9). On

Figure 5.9   Photograph of Jeffrey Vallance forging a copy of the Holy Lance.

30 October 1992, he brought it as close to the original in the Hofburg as he could, and, in the Josefplatz in Vienna, he performed his own renditions of several rituals that had been associated with the lance in various contexts in the late Middle Ages:[14] (1) He touched various rings to its tip; (2) He used it to stab six holes in each of several pieces of a cloth; (3) He dipped it in an ornamental chalice full of Austrian wine, which he subsequently drank; and (4) He held it aloft as he recited the Lord's Prayer in German. In his later comment on this performance Vallance suggests that he suspects the only photographic documentation of the performance was its accidental inclusion in a Japanese family's snapshots. He admits that he looked to see that none of the palace guards were watching – fearing their displeasure at seeing an inebriated man brandishing a weapon. He further volunteers that he had learned the words of the Lord's Prayer in German as a child while he attended Lutheran grade school (Vallance 1994).

This performance spawned further works as well as exhibitions and writings on them.[15] By 1994 Vallance had made three copies of the lance. In 1998 he presented the documentation on his lance project as mixed-media work on paper (Figure 5.10). On a sheet resembling an archival source or page torn from some early historian's notebook, he has dissected the lance into its constituent parts, all of which he has identified with arrows

The HOLY LANCE of LONGINUS

a.k.a. die Heilige Lanze, the Spear of Destiny, the Romphea, and the Spear of Saint Maurice

Figure 5.10 Montage by Jeffrey Vallance, *The Holy Lance of Longinus.*

and labels in longhand. Thus he continues the artifactuality of the object. On his website Vallance maintains the factuality summarizing the received history of the lance and the beliefs that enshroud it, beginning with the account in John 19:34 and ending with reports that it had been responsible for the fall of the Berlin Wall and the (first) Gulf War. We see faithful retellings along with subtle artistic addenda and sleight-of-hand manipulations that ironically may here stand unveiled for scrutiny more so than the inaccuracies and inconsistencies of the television documentary. Typical of the kinds of happenings that Vallance stages is the still photograph of his lance that appears to capture the kind of blur caused by an object being moved while the shutter of the camera was open for a longer time, to which he adds the provocative comment "showing mysterious movement after the film was developed," a comment that one must ponder for a moment in order to catch both its innate truth and his irony. From his research, Vallance knew that history had already produced multiple holy lances, and that the question of which one was "real" had long been a concern. Vallance states that he made copies to be put into circulation in order to "keep this process going," venturing that perhaps in five hundred years they may be confused with the "original." Vallance sees his work as an extension of the historical process, a further contamination of myths that are still evolving, or as little tweaks of reality. In the processes of making things make sense he has often "infiltrated" – a word he himself has used – certain (sub)cultures. He likewise allows recipients of his work to find the connections or make the meanings while he sits back observing, recording, or commenting on his diverse audiences – effecting a reversal of the roles of the (art) historian/critic and the artist. In so doing he opens windows onto cultural processes that have (re-)validated art objects or religious artifacts as icons both in the past and the present. Through his provocative humor and self-irony as well as his accepting treatment of viewers who gaze at the Holy Lance or his lance, perceiving an array of vastly different objects and meanings, he may have facilitated more critical thinking than any television documentary, book or website.

In conclusion, it is noteworthy that the lance appears to fulfill two somewhat opposite needs. Since the lance was believed to be imbued with superior, superhuman, supernatural powers, it could easily serve as a fictional surrogate for super weapons such as nuclear bombs, stealth fighters, or cruise missiles. On the other hand, since it was a simple, hand-held implement, of a kind used by many cultures, it could satisfy primal needs for expressing dominance, anger, or aggression through tests of prowess in hand-to-hand combat. Much of popular medievalism today – whether in medieval festivals, Renaissance fairs, or other manifestations of such social anachronisms currently in vogue – capitalizes on notions of distant periods dominated by violence of a most primitive variety in which individual right was defined by individual might. In all our examples, individuals and groups have renarratized the lance in order to (re)appropriate it for new interests and purposes. In other words, they have extended the story of the lance by writing new chapters to its history or by fashioning new contexts through pictures. These addenda expanded the lance's field of intertextual references and thus altered the whole. Initially the lance was sanctified because it was the lance "that pierced the side of Christ," subsequently it became "the spear of destiny." The Christian history of the lance – in the New Testament and the Middle Ages – was thereby relegated to a few mere episodes in its history. As such, the lance as a cultural icon was effectively de-Christianized. Further, it became an object that was of and by itself potent, not by virtue of its connections with Christ and the Crucifixion. The lance was fashioned as an all-powerful, transhistorical instrument in much the same way that certain kinds of crystals, knots, or herbs are now believed by many to possess supernatural powers. Certain dangers lie at the root of religions and entertainments that play with feelings of fear and admiration for people and things that are naturally yet inexplicably potent, as well as the corresponding disdain for that which is constructed as naturally weak and vulnerable. In the work of Vallance we see the lance as a privileged site for the elucidation of the multiple processes at stake in the making of icons.

Notes

1. On the lance in Nuremberg see: Schier and Schleif (2005).
2. Treasury-Schatzkammer: The Holy Lance. *Kunsthistorisches Museum Vienna: The Holy Lance*. 1998. 25 January 2000. http://www.khm.at/khm.at/khm/staticE/page477.html
3. Cabrera. Amazon.de, auf einen Blick: Spear of Destiny 6 May 2000. 7 October 2000. http://www.amazon.de/Spear-Destiny-Occult-Behind-Pierced/dp/0877285470.
4. The Holy Lance. *The UnMuseum - The Holy Lance*. 22 February 2002. http://www.unmuseum.org/spear.htm
5. "The Holy Lance." *Catholic Encyclopedia: The Holy Lance*. 1999. 10 January 2002. http://www.newadvent.org/cathen/08773a.htm
6. 10 September 2000. http://user.fastinet.net/kalogonis/index/lance.htm
7. *History of the ISCE*. 24 March 2002. http://www.hollow-earth.org/history.html
8. *Study Antichrist through Study of Hitler - Christian Updates - New World Order*. 24 March 2002. http://www.cuttingedge.org/n1017.html
9. Fisher (1996) points to the creation of hypermemory based on and enabled through forgetting. Memory is linked to the body and through the process of disembodiment, memory is left behind in the virtualization of reality. This makes possible the "total presence of absolute recall."
10. K. Webb. *The Spear of Destiny. A Relic for the Gothic Earth*. 16 October 2000. http://www.kargatane.com/souls/speardestiny.html
11. S. Crisman. *Lara Croft and the Spear of Destiny*. 11 November 2000. http://trarchive.ctimes.net/spear.html; 24 March 2002. http://www.slyngel.dk/tomb/auth-crisman.html. The makers of the Lara Croft computer games took up the motif of the lance in their *Tomb Raider V: The Chronicles*.
12. Whelehan and Sonnet (1997) point out that the real-life versions of *Tank Girl*, who participated in look-alike contests sponsored by lesbians who had appropriated this popular comic book figure from the late 1980s, were considered particularly threatening by heterosexual males who composed the primary readership of this adult comic.
13. As this article goes to press the numbers of productions on the lance have greatly increased. Atlantic Productions broadcast *The Spear of Jesus* in the US on the Discovery Channel in April 2003, and *The Spear of Christ* on the BBC's Channel Two in May 2003. Both offer a pseudoscientific analysis in an attempt to verify the lance's origins and history. Tellux produced a German-language documentary for Zweites Deutsche Fernsehen in 2004.
14. For discussions of the historical occurrences of these rituals associated with the Holy Lance see: Schier and Schleif (2005).
15. Of particular interest is the pamphlet by J. Vallance (1992) *Die Heilige Lanze und das Schweißtuch der Veronika*, Vienna, published on the occasion of the exhibition LAX at the Krinzinger Galerie, containing not only Vallance's own writings but an excellent essay by Ralph Rugoff, "Throwing the Spear of Destiny, Blindfolded, at a Distance of Fifty Meters, towards a Shuddering Shroud: Jeffrey Vallance's Unholy Histories."

References

Anderson, K. (1995). *Hitler and the Occult*. Amherst, NY: Prometheus Books.
Apter, E. and W. Pietz, eds. (1993). *Fetishism as Cultural Discourse*. Ithaca, NY and London: Cornell University Press.
Buechner, H. A. and W. Bernhard. (1989). *Adolf Hitler and the Secrets of the Holy Lance*. (2nd ed.) Metairie, LA: Thunderbird Press.

Fisher, J. (1996). The Postmodern Paradiso: Dante, Cyberpunk, and the Technosophy of Cyberspace. In D. Porter (ed.), *Internet Culture*, 110–28. New York and London: Routledge.

Fiske, J. (1989). *Understanding Popular Culture*. Boston: Unwin Hyman.

Greenwald, R. (1996). *The Spear of Golgotha*. Mareeba, Australia: Montrose Forfar.

Groebner, V. (1999). Der öffentliche Leichnam, reproduziert: Der Gekreuzigte und Medien städtischer Gewalt. *Micrologus: Natura, scienze e società medievali* 7: 383–403.

Herbert, J. (1999). *The Spear*. London: Pan Books.

Jeffrey, R. and A. Hunt. (2000). *The Spear of Tyranny*. Nashville, TN: Word Publishing.

Kahsnitz, R. (1982). Das Ardennenkreuz: Eine crux gemmata aus karolingischer Zeit. In R. Pörtner (ed.), *Das Schatzhaus der deutschen Geschichte*, 131–53. Düsseldorf and Vienna: Econ.

Kelly, C. (1995). *The Aryan*. Nashville: Thomas Nelson.

Lee, E., W. Simpson, and D. Spiegle. (1995). *Indiana Jones and the Spear of Destiny*, vol. 4. Edina, MN: Spotlight.

Merback, M. B. (1998). *The Thief, the Cross and the Wheel: Pain and the Spectacle of Punishment in Medieval and Renaissance Europe*. Chicago: Chicago University Press.

Peirce, C. S. (1993). One, Two, Three: Fundamental Categories of Thought and of Nature. *Writings of Charles S. Peirce*, vol. 5, 242–47. Bloomington: Indiana University Press.

Ravenscroft, T. (1982). *The Spear of Destiny: The Occult Power Behind the Spear Which Pierced the Side of Christ*. York Beach, ME: Samuel Weiser.

Ravenscroft, T. and T. Wallace-Murphy. (1990). *The Mark of the Beast: The Continuing Story of the Spear of Destiny*. York Beach, ME: Samuel Weiser.

Schier, V. and C. Schleif. (2005). Seeing and Singing, Touching and Tasting the Holy Lance: The Power and Politics of Embodied Religious Experiences in Nuremberg 1424–1524. In N. Bell, C. Cluver, and N. H. Petersen (eds.), *Signs of Change: Transformations of Christian Traditions in the West, Representation and Interpretation in the Arts 1000–2000*, 401–26. Amsterdam: Rodopi.

Still, B. (1992). *Legend of the Holy Lance: A Novel*. Lafayette, LA: Huntingdon House.

Tomaselli, K. (1999). *Appropriating Images: The Semiotics of Visual Representation*. Højbjerg: Intervention Press.

Vallance, J. (1992). *Die Heilige Lanze und das Schweißtuch der Veronika*. Book accompanying exhibition LAX. Vienna: Krinzinger Galerie.

———. (1994). *The World of Jeffrey Vallance*. Los Angeles: Art Issues.

Whelehan, I. and E. Sonnet. (1997). Regendered Reading: Tank Girl and Postmodernist Intertextuality. In D. Carthmell et al. (eds.), *Trash Aesthetics: Popular Culture and its Audience*, 31–47. London and Chicago: Pluto Press.

Zickmund, S. (1997). Approaching the Radical Other: The Discursive Culture of Cyberhate. In Steven G. Jones (ed.), *Virtual Culture: Identity and Communication in Cybersociety* 185–205. London: Sage Publications.

Comics

Benitez, J., P. Steigerwald, J. Weems, and T. Wengler. (2000). *Spear of Destiny*. The Darkness 15–18. Los Angeles: Top Cow.

Lee, E., W. Simpson, D. and Spiegle. (1995). *Indiana Jones and the Spear of Destiny*. 4 vols. Milwaukie, OR: Dark Horse Comics.

THE SEMIOTICS OF CULTURAL ICONS: THE EXAMPLE OF BRITANNIA

David Scott

Semiotics of the National Icon

National icons are complex signs, combining iconic, indexical, and symbolic functions. Taking these categories in the sense adumbrated by Charles Sanders Peirce (1960: 156–73), Britannia, as an icon, may be said to be *iconic* in that she resembles her object, the state of Great Britain (the way in which she does this will be discussed further); as an *index*, she points to the country or to those aspects of it (its constitution, economic status, naval or colonial power, etc.) that are relevant in a given context; as a *symbol*, she becomes a conventional sign, on par with other conventional signs (the Crown, the Royal Coat of Arms, etc.), which are read by their interpretants as referring unproblematically to their immediate objects. Like all signs, national icons such as Britannia are susceptible to two sorts of semiotic manipulation. In their official capacity, as controlled by government or other approved agencies, they aspire to a certain fixity and stasis, one that ensures both their immediate recognition (as signs referring to what Peirce describes as an "immediate object") and the control of their *meaning*. To help ensure this relative monovalence and fixity, their agreed attributes are closely guarded and rigorously observed. Furthermore, the icon itself is embodied in forms – coins, seals, statues and monuments, printed images such as postage stamps – that are officially commissioned or approved, and that cannot legally be tampered with. However, the potential multivalence and versatility of any icon immediately becomes released when it is removed from a controlled context and inserted in a field of wider reference. In such a situation, the dynamic potential of the icon is unleashed, particularly in association with other images with which it may come into contact in its unofficial context. This is especially true in posters, caricatures, or other satirical images, whose prime function is precisely to multiply the suggestive connotations of the icon, to humorous, subversive, or parodic effect. The corpus of images of Britannia that will be studied in this chapter will be largely divided into these two domains: official or conventional images – coins, stamps, sculpture – and satirical or subversive images – caricatures and cartoons. But before moving on to examine this corpus in detail, I make here a few more remarks on the semiotic complexity of the icon.

Although, in theory, icon, index, and symbol, as forms and categories of sign, seem to operate on a descending scale of verisimilitude or naturalness, in fact they all are fundamentally artificial signs, flavored with a strong dosage of conventional seasoning. If an icon is a sign that resembles its object, one might ask what is the "object" that Britannia resembles? An armor-clad woman, clutching a shield emblazoned with the Union Jack flag and brandishing a trident – does she resemble anything more than herself? The Britannia icon manages to escape this congenital tautology, however, by using two *indexical* strategies: she includes within her regalia other signs – for example, that of the national flag, the Union Jack – that point to the country with which she is associated; and she herself as a figure is usually placed in a minimal context – waves or stretch of shoreline with naval warship in the offing – signs that are also indexes of the country she represents (Britain the island maritime power). The trident, originally associated with Poseidon/Neptune, offers a further indexical alibi, reinforcing the icon's maritime association and mythical dimension. The viewer's ability to interpret these symbols correctly is of course itself a function of the interpretant's reference to what Peirce describes as "collateral experience," which can include education, prior knowledge, and the other influences that ensure the passage of meaning in a given cultural context.

A feature of the indexical elements or functions operative within the icon is their propensity to move in two directions: inwards, to reinforce the iconic status of the sign of which they are attributes; and outwards, to point to other connections that reinforce or complexify the identity of the central icon. In "official" representations of the national icon, it is the inward dynamic that is preponderant; when the icon is used in more open – satirical, humorous, or other – contexts, it is the outward dynamic that predominates, stretching as it were the icon's attributes to embrace connotations or situations that lie beyond its normal functions. It is this tension between official and unofficial indexical propensities within the icon that makes it such a rich cultural sign, enabling it to express both a certain continuity and new areas of meaning and interpretation. A rich icon is thus one that can survive centuries of change, contriving to remain relevant to varying circumstances while retaining its own fundamental identity. To do this it needs to be recognizable as a more or less conventional sign or *symbol*, while at the same time making its visual attributes as an *icon* work effectively in different contexts to *indicate* specific meanings or associations that go beyond its essential attributes. In other words, national icons are most successful when they exploit fully their triple semiotic status.

Origins of the Britannia Icon in Classical Mythology

The monarch, crown, national flag, figure of Saint George, and the royal coat of arms (with lion and unicorn), were all well established as English national symbols before the allegorical figure of Britannia began to make an appearance in the late sixteenth and early seventeenth centuries. It was the accession of James VI of Scotland to the throne of England in 1603, uniting the two countries as Great Britain, together with the growing might of English naval power throughout the Elizabethan and Stuart ages that perhaps most motivated the cultivation of a new national symbol, Britannia. Of course, Britannia had already been represented in Roman sculpture from as far back as the first century AD – as in the bas-relief of the time of the Emperor Claudius excavated in Asia Minor (Warner 1985) – and had appeared on Roman British coins dating from the first century AD (Figure 6.1). But there is a certain ambiguity attached to such early representations. In the former, Britannia, a fallen warrior woman, is seized by Claudius, while in

Figure 6.1 Roman coin, Antonius Pius (AD 138–161), British Museum.

the Roman coins, the seated female figure should probably be interpreted as Rome ensconced on English shores rather than as a national deity. The icon thus only began to be promoted in a positive, nationalist light in the early modern period, when Britain's imperial power was growing in a way that made comparison with that of the Roman Empire possible. Thus, various engraved images of Britannia begin to appear on title pages or in illustrations in later sixteenth- and early seventeenth-century texts, such as William Camden's *Britannia* of 1607, or Henry Peacham's *Minerva Britannica* of 1612.[1] The Camden image (Figure 6.2), in which Britannia, armed with two staves and protected by a shield, sits on a rocky shore with Elizabethan or Jacobean-style galleons cruising in the offing, already presents a near complete repertory of the deity's attributes.

The Romanized but nationalist adaptation of Britannia continued apace in the later seventeenth century, when the attributes of Athena/Minerva, goddess of wisdom and guardian of the state, with her plumed helmet, and of Poseidon/Neptune, god of the sea, with his trident, were incorporated into Britannia's regalia, along with the Union flag that emblazoned her shield (the George cross superimposed on that of Saint Andrew). The association with Britannia of the austere virtues of the classical deities Athena and Minerva brought to her not only the masculine qualities of steadfastness, courage, and strength, but also rekindled other associations pertaining to female images of English heroism, whether those of the

Figure 6.2 William Camden, *Britannia*, 1607, British Library.

ancient Briton, Queen Boadicea, or that of the virgin Queen Elizabeth I, Gloriana.[2] The Britannia medal (Figure 6.3) designed by the Dutch engraver John Roettiers in 1667, for which Charles II's mistress, Frances Stuart, Duchess of Richmond, is said to have posed, followed in 1672 by the engraving of Britannia's image on farthings and halfpennies, and, later, pennies (Figure 6.4), underlined not only Britannia's broadening

Figure 6.3   Britannia Medal, 1667, British Museum.

Figure 6.4   Penny coin, 1897
(Victoria's Diamond Jubilee year).

prestige as a national symbol, but also her association with currency and commerce.[3] So, for example, the olive branch, symbol of peace, that Britannia holds in the 1667 medal, marks not only the Treaty of Breda, which it was cast to celebrate, but also symbolizes the peace that in more general terms is the prerequisite for profitable trading, especially between maritime powers such as Britain and the Netherlands. It is also of course associated with Athena who, according to myth, was the first to present her city, Athens, with an olive tree, a descendent of which still grows on the Acropolis.

The seventeenth century thus marks for Britannia as icon a period of semiotic consolidation and regularization: in it are established her essential attributes and the iconic components that give expression to them – fortitude (armor, including the Athenian helmet), imperial status (England and Scotland, and their increasing colonial territories, united under the national flag, the Union Jack that emblazons Britannia's buckler), maritime power (trident), commercial enterprise (ships in background), pacific intentions when not threatened (olive branch), and island independence (the rocky shore). The continuity of the icon and its associated attributes is attested to by the stability of its representation in subsequent official images and artifacts, whether coins, banknotes, or, from the 1850s, postage stamps, from the Stuart period to the present day. Like the image of Britannia herself, confined within the plates of her armor, the official icon is *engraved* in an indelible outline, frozen into a pose and attributes that have remained consistently apposite, until the end of the twentieth century at least, in their range of reference. The way this rigidity is softened and Britannia's potentially human qualities – or failings – can become evident will be seen in the next section, in which exploration of her image shifts from official contexts to the more subversive sphere of cartoon and satirical engraving or to the more creative sphere of artistic representation. Such contexts expose both Britannia's semiotic ambiguity and the icon's flexibility to varying and multiple interpretations. These latter remain of course, even at their most perverse, dependent upon Britannia's profile as understood within official or standard representations of her.

Britannia's Heyday in the Eighteenth and Nineteenth Centuries

The continuing eighteenth-century growth of Britain's naval and colonial might was marked by an increasingly general and confident use of Britannia as an icon of national propaganda, as many examples of official and memorial sculpture of the period attest. In Westminster Abbey, Roubiliac's remarkable memorials to military chiefs such as the Duke of Argyll (1748) and Sir Peter Warren (1753) offer variations on the Britannia theme that are particularly interesting in the way, reflecting an artistic temperament or aesthetic effect, they show how a national icon may be subtly modified. In the memorial to Argyll, who served as a soldier in Marlborough's and other successful campaigns, the French sculptor has bestowed on Britannia, who appears on a bas-relief adjacent to the more fully three-dimensional form of Minerva, many of the attributes (bared breast, relaxed pose, Phrygian bonnet on a spear) that will later characterize the symbol of the French Republic, Marianne. In the Warren monument, as befits the memorial of a vice-admiral, Britannia makes an appearance front stage and in full scale, though even here the sensuous presence of her body, in flowing draperies with plunging neckline, takes precedence over the diminutive flag-emblazoned shield that looks more like a chocolate box than a buckler – an idea reinforced by the exquisitely carved horn of plenty that spills over with sacrificial lamb in baroque extravagance to her left side.

Perhaps, though, the most stupendous of all commemorative projects involving Britannia was John Flaxman's proposal of 1799 for a pillar commemorating Nelson's victory at the Battle of the Nile to be raised on Observatory Hill in Greenwich.[4] Never executed, it would have consisted of a colossal statue of Britannia, 230 feet high, mounted on a gigantic plinth inscribed "Britannia by Divine Providence Triumphant." Flaxman also produced a silver vase (Figure 6.5) commemorating Nelson's naval victory at Trafalgar in 1805, on one side of which appears Britannia Triumphant, holding Winged Victory in her right hand, her left resting on a shield embossed with the British lion, and, among many monuments, one to Lord Nelson, whose circular base is flanked by Britannia and the British lion. Britannia's profound association with British naval victories was also, of course, since 1740, consolidated by the success of James Thompson's poem "Rule Britannia," which, set to music by Thomas Arne, figured as the finale of his masque *Alfred*. The song – "Rule Britannia, Britannia rules the waves/Britons never, never, never shall be slaves" – became in effect, from the nineteenth century, a kind of national anthem, sometimes used as an alternative to the more purely royalist song "God save the King," which was, moreover, French in origin.

As some of the above examples show, with Britannia's establishment as a major national icon in her own right, she increasingly appeared, in both sculpture and caricature, in association with other national icons, in particular the British lion. This animal, which provides stately transport for Britannia in Baron Marochetti's 1867 memorial to Field Marshal Lord Clyde in Waterloo Place, London, also appears rampant in many images of Britannia in eighteenth- and nineteenth-century caricatures. In George Cruikshank's etching of 1819, *DEATH or LIBERTY! Or Britannia & the Virtues of the Constitution in danger of violation from the grt. Political*

Figure 6.5 John Flaxman (1755–1826), Trafalgar Vase, 1805–1806, Victoria & Albert Museum.

Libertine, Radical reform (Figure 6.6), the Lion of Loyalty ambles up to assist Britannia, who, as Guardian of Religion and Monarchy (she wears around her waist the royal garter inscribed *Dieu et mon Droit*), tries to defend herself with the Sword of the Laws against Radical Reform, whose thinly masked figure, armed with a pike crowned with tricolor rosette and Phrygian bonnet, barely disguises the worst aspects of the French Revolution, whose grisly consequences follow in his train. Meanwhile, in Gillray's 1808 cartoon, *Leo Britannicus* has been let off his leash to thwart Napoleon's progress in the Peninsula War.

But it is when she is left to her own devices, in the face of Napoleonic aggression or that of Britain's own ministers, that the Britannia of caricature and the satirical cartoon becomes most human and vulnerable. Thus in James Gillray's etching of 1783, *A New ADMINISTRATION, or – The State Quacks ADMINISTRING* (Figure 6.7), the political rivals Lord North and Charles James Fox join forces in an unholy alliance to "serve Britannia" by administering an enema. Crawling on all fours and clutching her abdomen in pain, Britannia has dropped and cracked her

Figure 6.6 George Cruikshank (1792–1878), DEATH or LIBERTY! Or Britannia and the Virtues of the Constitution in danger of <u>Violation</u> from the gr^t Political Libertine, <u>Radical reform!</u> 1 December 1819.

Figure 6.7 James Gillray (1757–1815), A *New ADMINISTRATION, or – The State Quacks ADMINISTRING*, etching with aquatint, 1 April 1783.

shield and uses her spear not as means of defense but as a support to her semirecumbent position, her lack of armor leaving her nether parts exposed to the dubious "administrations" of the "State Quacks." Gillray's strategy, in stripping Britannia of her martial attributes, or in other ways damaging or neutralizing them, has the effect of demythologizing her as an icon, rendering her as vulnerable as any woman to male aggression. In this case, Britannia's undignified position and the exposure even of her innermost bowels to the ministrations of temporal power, constitute what is tantamount to an official rape, one which Gillray no doubt calculated would have a powerful shock effect, playing as it does both on the idea of rape as a human act and as symbolic defilement.

The play on the word *administer* in both its medical and political senses is also implicitly exploited by Gillray in a cartoon of 1804, *Britannia between DEATH and the DOCTORS*, in which a sick Britannia is left exposed by her incompetent ministers (Pitt, Addington, and Fox) to the surreptitious sexual and political attack of Napoleon, whose skinny figure lurks behind her bed curtains, brandishing a spear. Britannia wears a cameo at her breast, bearing the image of King George III, whose health, not to say sanity, was also a matter of grave concern at that time. The olive branch Britannia has let slip is that of the recent Peace of Amiens, and signals the renewal of hostilities that was soon to take place between Britain and France. Once again, the imminent rape or death of Britannia, as both woman and icon, is conjured up in this image, as it had been to even more ghastly effect by Gillray in his *PHANTASMAGORIA: -* Scene *– Conjuring up an Armed Skeleton* of 1803, in which the ghost of Britannia emerges from a cauldron brewed by the king's ministers dressed as witches. Here Britannia is not only stripped of all her symbolic attributes except the shield with Union Jack that serves, as it were, to identify her, but also of all her clothes and her flesh. The Gallic cock looks on, no doubt crowing, from his dunghill, sporting a revolutionary rosette that matches that of Charles James Fox. This dialogue of icons (British versus French) enables Gillray to express in visual shorthand the clash of ideologies at stake.

This sort of dialogue or dramatization of national icons is also exploited by Gillray in a cartoon of 1805, *ST GEORGE and the DRAGON – a design for an Equestrian Statue, from the Original in Windsor Castle*, in which George III himself comes to rescue Britannia from assault by the Napoleonic dragon. Once again, Britannia, divested of her martial attributes except the shield, itself fallen beneath the virile coils of the French monster's tail, appears as a tragic heroine, while George III, mounted on a rearing horse, looks like a parody, not only of the English patron saint, but also of those martial paintings of Napoleon by Louis David: the visual/intertextual message here then is that of British chivalry, despite its unlikely royal horseman, outclassing that of its French model.

But Gillray's image also implies a parody both of commemorative sculpture and national icons in general, the monarch included. For the cartoon's title underlines the absurdity of the idea of erecting an equestrian statue to George III, whose all too human failings, not least his bouts of insanity, had given rise to much public and political concern, especially at a time of great national danger (the Napoleonic wars). Such subversive implications are largely toned down later in the century, in particular during Victoria's long and stable reign.

When turning to look at Victorian representations of Britannia, in particular when they appear signed by John Tenniel in the satirical magazine *Punch* (1841–1892), it is striking that she never appears in a position or pose of vulnerability. With the Napoleonic Wars behind her and a largely peaceful century ahead under the reign of Queen Victoria (1837–1901), Britannia can afford to stand erect and unarmed, robed in a bland and matronly dress, with nothing but the Athenian helmet, and occasionally the Union Jack–emblazoned buckler, to remind us of her martial prowess. The austere purity of her attire attests of course to her moral as well as military superiority, as in a Tenniel cartoon of 1878 in which she disdains to clasp the bloodied hand of Turkey in the aftermath of the Bulgarian massacres. In another Tenniel vignette, *'Too late!'* of 1885, erect and undefeated, sword still drawn, Britannia nevertheless laments the failure of British troops to relieve General Gordon and prevent his assassination at Khartoum. Britannia's moral authority is also exerted over Queen Victoria herself, as in another Tenniel cartoon, *Queen Hermione* in *Punch* in which, in 1865, she draws back the curtain on an enthroned Victoria to reveal the monarch dressed for state and appearing in public for the first time after a long period of mourning the death of her consort Prince Albert in 1861. The relative semiotic economy of nineteenth-century representations of Britannia, even in parodic and satirical contexts, attests thus both to the power of the nation she symbolizes and the prestige and integrity she continues to enjoy as a national icon. This uniformity will be lost in the modern period as the vicissitudes of a tempestuous century threaten the fortunes of a declining British Empire and, in the process, undermine British national self-confidence. But before going on to explore this latter development, a brief comparison will be made of Britannia's symbolic function with other national icons.

Britannia and Other National Symbols

The relationship between Britannia and other British national icons – Saint George, John Bull, the British lion, the head or figure of the monarch, the crown – is much too vast and complex a subject to deal with here, so I shall restrict myself in this section to a few comments on those national icons – in particular John Bull and the British lion – which, in their masculine or aggressive character attributes, most plausibly supplement or complement those of Britannia. As previous examples have shown, the British lion, in the eighteenth century, represented the aggressive, masculine side of British power, defending British interests at home and overseas, and also increasingly standing for British commerce and trading interests. In addition, the lion's heraldic origin and prominent profile (not least its conspicuous presence in the royal coat of arms) and its long history as a British national symbol, will assure its continuing use in many official forms – seals, figureheads, and stamps, for example, as we shall see.

John Bull, on the other hand, is a more recent invention, and one more vivid and specific in character. He was born in John Arbuthnot's allegorical satire of 1712, *The History of John Bull*, and was particularly popular in the nineteenth- and twentieth-century political cartoons. Incarnating essential traits of the British character, he was "an honest, plain dealing Fellow, Cholerick, Bold, and of very inconstant Temper" (Arbuthnot 1976: 9), commonsensical, cheerful, trustworthy, and fearless. Although described as a "clothier," he has the air of a sportsman and gentleman farmer: he is normally presented dressed in riding coat and riding boots and, reflecting the British enthusiasm for and promotion of boxing, is often depicted defending British rights or interests with his fists. Thus a cartoon by John Leech of 1846 has John Bull staring down his diminutive American opponent, ignoring his raised fists and horse whip, saying, "What? You young yankee-noodle, strike your own father!" While in another of 1899, this time by John Tenniel, it is the Boer who picks the fight, to be told by John Bull, jacket off and sleeves rolled, "As you *will* fight, you shall have it. *This* time it's a fight to the finish."

Not only does John Bull thus spare Britannia many of the dirtier or manlier tasks of defending Britain's interests (in a cartoon in *Punch* of 1859, he guards Queen Victoria's gunpowder against any French imperial aggression), but is also co-opted to face out national humiliations. A deep sense of the comic, another British characteristic embodied by John Bull, thus enables him to survive absurd or undignified situations without fundamentally losing respect, something that, as some of Gillray's cartoons showed, was much more difficult for Britannia. Thus in a Tenniel cartoon of 1876, John Bull is tossed by an American bull, as cheap meat imported from the United States played havoc with British farming in the agricultural depression of the 1870s. He is also prepared to appear as a comic figure in attempting to manage certain delicate colonial situations, as in a Linley Sambourne cartoon of 1888, in which, in army uniform and pith helmet, he is seen "Wooing the African Venus." Meanwhile in a Tenniel

caricature of 1879, "A black 'White Elephant,'" he is confronted with the problem of what to do with the captured Zulu warrior king Cetshwayo.

Britannia in the Twentieth Century

A glance at British stamps up to the end of George VI's reign in 1952 (that is, up to the explosion of commemorative issues that has characterized the reign of Elizabeth II) shows a roughly even distribution of images among Britannia, St. George, and the British lion. Although since its introduction by Sir Rowland Hill in 1840, British stamps have primarily been identified by the royal head (as in the famous Penny Black of 1840, which set the pattern for British definitive stamps for the next 150 years), some British colonial stamps from the 1850s used Britannia as an alternative (Figure 6.8). The British lion first appeared on a British stamp in 1911, the first definitive of George V's reign, and reappeared on the first British commemorative stamp, issued in 1924 to mark the British Empire Exhibition. St. George followed in 1929 when he appeared on a large-format, high-value (£1) stamp commemorating the Universal Postal Union Congress in London, and again in 1951 when he appeared on a ten shilling stamp in the second high-value definitive series of George VI's reign. Meanwhile, the royal coat of arms had appeared, beautifully adapted by Edmund Dulac, on the first George VI high-value definitive series in 1937. Britannia herself first appeared on a British stamp in 1912 (Figure 6.9), where she graced the four high-value stamps that were to be used until the end of George V's reign in 1936. In this design by

Figure 6.8   Recess Perkins, Bacon & Co, Barbados definitive stamp 1852.

Figure 6.9   Bertram Mackennal, George V definitive stamp, 1913–1936.

Bertram Mackennal, an erect Britannia, right hand thrusting forward the trident, the left bearing the shield emblazoned with the Union Jack, is conveyed over the waves by horses following the direction of the gaze of George V, which, exceptionally but to great dynamic effect, looks out of the stamp to the left rather than rightwards into it. Britannia first appeared on British commemorative stamps in 1951, when the logo of the Festival of Britain, designed by Abram Games in 1948, was adapted to a 4d stamp by the same designer (Figure 6.10); an alternative design, also incorporating the head of Britannia, was produced by Edmund Dulac for the 2 1/2p stamp. A 1990 souvenir sheet marking the 150th anniversary of the first postage stamp included, along with the new 20p stamp, a reproduction of the Penny Black set in a fine engraving of Britannia. Britannia's most recent stamp appearance was in 1993 when the highest value (£10) definitive (Figure 6.11), designed by B. Craddock, was issued. In this exceptionally large format stamp, she rules in full glory over what remains of the British Empire, upholding the value of a by now much-devalued Sterling.

The gradual decline of the British Empire after the First World War was naturally reflected in various political and satirical cartoons, in particular in *Punch*, where Bernard Partridge took up the mantle left by Sir John Tenniel – as in the cartoon *Her Protector* of 1935 – in which the British lion tries to stay Britannia's decline through the crises of the 1930s. But

Figure 6.10   Abram Games (1914–1998), Festival of Britain commemorative stamp, 1951.

Figure 6.11   B. Craddock, £10 definitive stamp, 1993.

relative British decline in colonial and economic power was compensated to some degree by other initiatives with which Britannia was connected. Royal yachts were named after Britannia from 1892 (the first British ship bearing this name, a naval one-hundred-gunner, having been launched in 1682) until that of the present queen, while the name also graced an advanced turbo-prop airliner of the 1950s, the *Bristol Britannia* (also known as the "Whispering Giant") and also, in the 1970s and 1980s, an airline. Most significantly of all, Britannia was chosen as the logo of the Festival of Britain, organized in 1951 (the centenary of the great Crystal Palace exhibition of 1851) to display to the postwar world Britain's achievements and promise in the fields of industry, technology, architecture, and design.

But it has perhaps been in the area of retail, communications, and popular culture – whether shops, fashion, music, or entertainment – that Britain has won the widest acclaim in the second half of the twentieth century. So, the "Cool Britannia" of the last decade is associated by many with Britpop music, London street fashion (the Union Jack as a design motif has been vital since the 1960s), trendy shops, television, and comedy. The British propensity towards comedy and comic self-deflation, evident at least since the time of John Bull, has permeated all aspects of contemporary cultural life. Thus, on the cover of the election-day issue of the *Sun* newspaper in June 1983, the outgoing prime minister, Margaret Thatcher, still bathing in the reflected glory of British victory in the Falkland Islands war, is presented on the front page as a caricatured reincarnation of Britannia (Warner 1985: 38–60). And even within such official media as postage stamps, a new, more relaxed approach to the icons representative of national identity is apparent. Thus, in two stamps, one English and the other French-designed, issued in 1994 to mark the completion of the Anglo-French Channel Tunnel (Figure 6.12), a comic-book British Empire lion reaches across the sea to shake hands

Figure 6.12 George Hardie and Jean-Paul Cousin, Channel Tunnel commemorative stamps, 1994.

with the Gallic cock, while in the French design, Britannia's red, white, and blue be-ringed hand touches that of Marianne, decorated, as one would expect, with the same colors in reverse, the *bleu, blanc, et rouge* of the French republican rosette. The increasing pressure in the European Union for states to readjust or harmonize their national icons in the light of major partner or collaborative ventures is a trend that will continue into the twenty-first century.

Conclusion

Social communities, whether small so-called primitive societies, or large, often multiracial nation-states, all tend to identify themselves through reference to certain privileged visual signs, whether the totems of tribal groups or the national icons of modern countries.[5] The function of such signs is, of course, as much to *differentiate* one society or country from another as it is to *identify* a given community. This double motivation is a consequence of the linguistic principle established by Saussure (1980), whereby signs are constituted as much within a system of differences as in connection with specific referents. Lévi-Strauss, in *La Voie des masques* (1979), has studied the implications of this thesis in the context of American Indian masks. The same point is made at any contemporary international gathering at which the flags of participating nations are displayed together. So, as I pointed out, Britannia's indexical relation as a sign to its referent Great Britain is only fully comprehensible with reference to the other icons it incorporates (in particular the national flag), to the extent that even in some eighteenth-century appearances (such as Roubiliac's Argyll monument), it can be difficult to differentiate Britannia from other allegorical types such as Minerva. The various ways in which a given national icon – flag, flower symbol, allegorical figure, saint, or other national type – may establish a more motivated indexical or iconic relationship with its object or referent is much facilitated by Peirce's analysis of the sign/object relation. For it is in this area – where qualities (colors, forms, shapes) and associations (mythological, geographical, historical) come into play in a decisive way – that the structure and function of cultural icons can be best understood. But, as Peirce stressed in relation to his triadic semiotic categories, *mobility* as much as stasis is the principle governing the play of signs: not only do the various icons within a national repertory refer as much to each other as to their object, but they also become modified in their interaction. This point serves to underline the law that operates in relation to all signs: all are potentially volatile, their ongoing vitality being necessarily predicated on variation and change. The way the principle of identity (stasis) interacts with that of difference (mobility) is one of the enduring fascinations of signs, in particular when enriched, as is the case with cultural icons such as Britannia, with multiple layers of historical and symbolic association. And never more so than in the contemporary period in which, as Baudrillard (1976) argues, culture has become recognized as being more a function of sign exchange than of a real relation with its object.

Notes

1. For a fuller survey of late Elizabethan and early Stuart representations of Britannia, see Strong (1980: 30–34).
2. For a fuller exploration of the symbolic significance of Athena's and Britannia's armor, in particular as it bears on the value of chastity, see Warner (1985: 250–51).
3. In David Mallet's and David Garrick's *Britannia. A Masque* (1759), the Genius as Recitativo states:

   Britannia! Sovereign queen of Isles!
   Where freedom reigns, where plenty smiles,
   Whence commerce spreads, with every gale,
   For every shore, her boundless sail –

4. A sketch by William Blake of the proposed monument is reproduced in Mace (1976: 50). Mace's book shows how national icons such as Nelson's Column and Trafalgar Square have become associated with both national celebration and militant political demonstration and debate.
5. The recent practice among football or rugby enthusiasts of painting their national flag on their faces when attending international matches is an interesting example of the way early or primitive tribal practices have become rehabilitated in modern society.

References

Arbuthnot, J. (1976). *The History of John Bull*. A. W. Bower and R. A. Erickson (eds.). Oxford: Clarendon Press. (Orig. pub. 1712.)
Baudrillard, J. (1976). *L'Echange symbolique et la mort*. Paris: Gallimard.
Berkovitz, P. and P. Macdonald. (1992). Le Pouvoir impérial: l'Empire britannique dans les dessins de *Punch* (1918–1939). *Matériaux pour l'histoire de notre temps* 28 (juillet–septembre).
Bindman, D., ed. (1979). *John Flaxman*. London: Thames & Hudson.
Bindman, D. and M. Baker. (1995). *Roubiliac and the Eighteenth-Century Monument: Sculpture as Theatre*. New Haven, CT and London: Yale University Press.
Hugget, F. E. (1978). *Victorian England as seen by 'Punch'*. London: Sidgwick & Jackson.
Lévi-Strauss, C. (1979). *La Voie des masques*. Paris: Plon.
Mace, R. (1976). *Trafalgar Square: Emblem of Empire*. London: Lawrence & Wishart.
Opie, R. (1985). *Rule Britannia: Trading on the British Image*. London: Viking.
Peirce, C. S. (1960). *Collected Papers*, vol. 2. C. Hartshorne and P. Weiss (eds.). Cambridge, MA: Belknap Press, Harvard University Press.
Saussure, F. de (1980). *Cours de linguistique générale*. Tullio de Mauro (ed.). Paris: Payot.
Scott, D. (1996). Marianne et Britannia se rencontrent: les icones nationales et la structure sémiotique du timbre-poste français et anglais, *l'image* II: 140–56.
Strong, R. (1980). *Britannia triumphans: Inigo Jones, Rubens and Whitehall Palace*. London: Thames & Hudson.

Toby, M. P. (1897). *The Queen and Mr Punch*. London: Bradbury, Agnew.

Warner, M. (1985). *Monuments and Maidens: The Allegory of the Female Form*. London: Weidenfeld & Nicolson.

Whinney, M. and R. Gunnis. (1967). *The Collection of Models by John Flaxman, R.A. at University College London: A Catalog and Introduction*. London: University of London, Athlone Press.

INDEX

Index

ABOUT THE CONTRIBUTORS

STEPHANIE A. GLASER is a postdoctoral research assistant at the Centre for the Study of the Cultural Heritage of Medieval Rituals at the University of Copenhagen. Her research and teaching centers on the nineteenth-century understanding of the Gothic cathedral in England, Germany, and France as well as the ideological and architectural connections between the Eiffel Tower and the cathedral.

HANS LUND is associate professor emeritus of Comparative Literature and the former head of Intermedia Studies at Lund University in Sweden. He is the author of *Text as Picture: Studies in the Literary Transformation of Pictures* (Lewiston, 1993; Swedish edition, 1982), *Impressionism and Literary Text* (1993, in Swedish) and a large number of essays on inter-mediality and literary criticism. He has edited *Intermediality: Interactions between Words, Images and Music* (2002, in Swedish), and is a co-editor of several anthologies on intermedia studies, one of them in English: *Interart Poetics: Essays on the Interrelations of the Arts and Media* (Rodopi, 1997).

FINN HAUBERG MORTENSEN has been professor in Scandinavian Literature at University of Southern Denmark (1991–2007) and chair of the Danish Institute for Upper Secondary Pedagogics (1998–2007). Since 2007 he has been professor in Scandinavian Literature at University of Copenhagen and chair of the Department of Scandinavian Studies and Linguistics. He has been a member of the Danish Academy of Sciences and Letters since 1997, a member of the Danish Research Council for the Humanities 1993–1999 and chair 1996–1999, and chair of the Society for Danish Language and Literature since 2001. Professor Mortenson was a research professor at Søren Kierkegaard Research Centre, Copenhagen University,

1994–1999, and a visiting professor at universities in the US (Berkeley), Japan (Kwansei Gakuin), and many European countries.

VOLKER SCHIER is co-director together with Corine Schleif of the international multimedia project "Opening the Geese Book" at the Arizona Center for Medieval and Renaissance Studies. He has authored two books and has published widely on medieval chant and on the music cultures in the city of Nuremberg around 1500. Corine Schleif and Volker Schier are currently working on a book about the history of the Holy Lance.

CORINE SCHLEIF has published over fifty articles on the social history of art, including studies on the motivations of religious patrons, self-representation, ritual participation, art historiography, and women's roles in art and its history. Her book *Donatio et memoria* appeared in 1990. *Katerina's Windows*, co-authored with Volker Schier, is currently in press at Penn State Press. She teaches medieval and Renaissance art at Arizona State University.

DAVID SCOTT holds a personal chair in French (Textual and Visual Studies) at Trinity College, Dublin. His books include *Pictorialist Poetics* (Cambridge University Press, 1988), *Paul Delvaux* (Reaktion Books, 1992), *European Stamp Design: A Semiotic Approach* (Academy Editions, 1995), *Semiologies of Travel* (Cambridge University Press, 2004) and *The Art and Aesthetics of Boxing* (University of Nebraska Press, 2008). His translation of Mallarmé's sonnets also appeared in 2008 (Exeter: Shearsman Books). He is currently completing a book entitled *Figures de l'affiche / Poetics of the Poster*.

ARNOLD SHEPPERSON (MA) was a PhD student in Culture, Communication and Media Studies at the University of KwaZulu-Natal, Durban, South Africa. His PhD research, which focuses on issues of safety in South African mines, is funded by the Safety in Mines Research Advisory Committee. He has published in semiotics, cultural theory, media, educational, and health issues. See *Critical Arts: A Journal of South-North Cultural and Media Studies*, Volume 22, Issue 2, 2008, for a special issue on Shepperson's life and work. Regrettably, Shepperson died in late 2006 before completing his PhD thesis.

KEYAN G. TOMASELLI is Professor in Culture, Communication and Media Studies at the University of KwaZulu-Natal, Durban, South Africa. Tomaselli has been a Fulbright Scholar and is the author of numerous papers and books on African cultural and media studies, including *The Cinema of Apartheid* (Smyrna Press, 1988), *Appropriating Images*

(Intervention Press, 1996), *Encountering Modernity: Twentieth Century South African Cinemas* (Rozenberg Publishers, 2006), *Writing in the san/d: Autoethnography in among Indigenous South Africans* (AltaMira Press, 2007) and *Where Global Contradictions are the Sharpest: Research Stories from the Kalahari* (Rozenberg, 2005). He also co-edited the book *Media, Democracy and Renewal in Southern Africa* (2001) and is the editor-in-chief of *Critical Arts: A Journal of South-North Cultural and Media Studies.*